HUNTINGTON BEACH
·CHRONICLES·

HUNTINGTON BEACH
· CHRONICLES ·
The Heart of Surf City

CHRIS EPTING

Charleston · London

THE
History
PRESS

Published by The History Press
Charleston, SC 29403
www.historypress.net

Front cover, top left: courtesy the Williams family; *bottom*: courtesy Marvin Carlberg.
Back cover, bottom: courtesy the Wentworth family.
All other images are from the author's collection.

First published 2014

Manufactured in the United States

ISBN 978.1.60949.534.3

Library of Congress CIP data applied for.

This collection is dedicated to everyone who banded together during the summer of 2013 to fight the Southern California Air Quality Management District (AQMD), which tried to ban beach bonfires in our city. We showed the scoundrels what happens when you pick a fight with us, but still, let's never take our eyes off them. For all of the heart so many of you showed, thank you.

Contents

PROLOGUE

Now I know why I live in this paradise called "Surf City."
Beautiful beaches, warm sand and plenty of tall green palm trees…
Ocean breezes keep us cool, and at the same time, these breezes permeate the air with the sweet smells of the ocean mixed with the hint of smoke from one of our many beach barbecuing pits.

Now mix in the many stories in our beautiful city. And like any city, we have our highs and lows, but it seems like our highs are higher and our lows are, with the help of our compassionate neighbors, not quite so low.

Thank you, Chris, for writing all of these amazing stories.

Well done, my friend!

DEAN O. TORRENCE

FOREWORD

The *Huntington Beach Independent* values Chris enough to ensure that his column is always on the front page. There he is, a picture of his head that appears to be dangling in space, and you can be almost certain that he will be accentuating the positive about someone. Someone, because his specialty is writing about people. His column has been devoted to "latching on to the affirmative" about his subjects and telling their unique stories throughout his writing career.

What sets Chris apart from other columnists I read are his need to always emphasize the positive side of his subject and his insatiable curiosity. These traits are responsible for his writing in some detail about a very wide range of subjects, not the least of which is the city of Huntington Beach.

When I first started reading Chris's work, I quickly became convinced that Huntington Beach is his hometown; it was later that I learned of his New York roots. He writes lovingly about so many aspects, past, present and future, of Huntington Beach.

In the articles herein, Chris tells us fascinating stories about the people who are the flesh and blood of this beach city. The man who runs the Beef Palace; a lady resident who portrayed Erin Walton (remember, "Goodnight, John Boy"); the Singing Goodtimers at the Senior Center; the pyrotechnician who provides the city's great Fourth of July fireworks; the operator of a beauty salon whose life revolves around honoring the troops; the Silcock couple who have adopted and cared for forty-three disabled and/or abused children over the past ten years; the local legend Bob Terry and family of Terry Buick, who helped put the city on the map; the 1976 Olympic swimming gold medalist Shirley Babashoff, now a mail carrier in the area; the multitude of performers like Janis Joplin and the Byrds who once entertained at the legendary Golden Bear—the list goes on and on and demonstrates the diversity of the fascinating subjects he continuously discovers and reveals to his readers through his unwavering curiosity.

Somehow, his lovely wife, Jean, and their two bright-eyed children, Charlie and Claire, are able to deal with all of these distractions and round out his caring family life.

If I tell the readers of this book any more, I will be spoiling the fun for them, so I'll close with this thought. It occurred before I had even met Chris, when I only knew him through reading his newspaper columns.

Whenever I pondered his columns, a passage in *The Great Gatsby* kept echoing in my mind. It is when Fitzgerald's narrator, Nick Carraway, says, upon first meeting Gatsby, that he had "one of those rare smiles with a quality of reassurance in it. It concentrated on you with an irresistible prejudice in your favor. It understood you just as far as you wanted to be understood, believed in you as you would like to believe in yourself, and assured you that it had precisely the impression of you that, at your best, you hoped to convey."

About two years ago, when I finally met Chris at an informal meeting in Alice's Breakfast in the Park, I realized why this passage had kept echoing through my mind. Happy reading.

RICHARD D. REINBOLT OF HUNTINGTON BEACH

ACKNOWLEDGEMENTS

Thank you to all those at the *Huntington Beach Independent* who have allowed me to write my "In the Pipeline" column over the years: Paul Anderson, Tony Dondero, John Canalis, Michael Miller, Alicia Lopez, Tom Johnson, Alisha Gomez, Vilma Hidalgo-Cruz and everyone else at the paper.

Thanks, as well, to Jerry Roberts and his team at The History Press and also to Richard Reinbolt and Dean Torrence for their kind words contained within this collection.

And of course, last but not least, thank you to my wife, Jean; son, Charles; daughter, Claire; and my mom for always reading the column first and sending me a note about it.

*I*NTRODUCTION

About seven years ago, Paul Anderson, an editor with the *Los Angeles Times*–published newspaper the *Huntington Beach Independent*, called to see if I might have any interest in writing a weekly column for the paper.

At that point, I'd written a couple of books about the city and was in the process of becoming sort of a de facto historian—speaking at luncheons, schools and other places in the area. Paul's offer intrigued me, as I'd long (secretly) dreamed of one day having my own column. But what was he interested in from my writing? "Anything," he said. "Go find stories. Dig up some interesting stuff. Have fun."

Little did Paul know how much his phone call would end up enhancing my life. See, the column (brilliantly named "In the Pipeline" by Paul to convey a sense of "coming news," as well as referencing surfing and oil, two major facets of Huntington Beach) forced me to do exactly what he suggested: find stories and have fun.

While I think (for the most part) that I've succeeded, there's been more to what I've experienced, week in, week out: painful stories of loss that needed to be told and poignant stories of personal challenges have helped balance the flow.

But it's all storytelling, and as newspapers shrink away and local communities find it harder to find things to read about where they live, the stories seem to become more important.

As of this writing, I still write and photograph my column each week, and it's an integral part of my life, both personally and professionally. The stories I've chosen for this collection reflect, in my opinion, more universal themes so that whether you're familiar with Huntington Beach or not, they will resonate with you.

You'll meet some amazing people in this book who live by codes that I hope would make any community proud to have them.

So if you're in the mood to let your mind wander and roam a bit, to experience some of the people and places I've been fortunate enough to encounter, then I invite you to pull up a cozy chair or sofa.

There are some stories I'd like to share with you.

Chapter 1

SURF CITY

THE WRIGHT STUFF

Welcome to "In the Pipeline." Each week, this column will reveal, illuminate or expose something interesting about Huntington Beach. Quirks, characters, issues, oddities and opinions that make up this city will all flow in the pipeline. You may know that I write books about history and popular culture that dig deep, and I'll bring the same sensibility to this column. Online, I'll include video, photos and other elements to help bring "In the Pipeline" to life. Comments and ideas are welcomed. It's a big city, and any help documenting it is appreciated.

Recently, I discovered a strange landmark: a black granite tombstone at Springdale Street and Warner Avenue, in the bushes behind the Arco station. Its text reads: "In recognition of Lloyd Wright's 94-foot-high sign tower that was to have been erected on this spot. Its defeat is symbolic of the democratic process in which we live. The people did not wish this sign tower to be erected as they felt it was not needed and would blight their community. Their wishes were heard and adhered to by the developer, Stanley Fann.—1970."

A sign tower? Lloyd Wright (aka Frank Lloyd Wright Jr.), son of arguably our country's most famous architect, and designer of the Hollywood Bowl and Wayfarers Chapel in Palos Verdes, among other Southern California treasures—here?

I grilled many locals. Nothing. The gas station manager by the tombstone? Oblivious. Poring over spools of microfilm at Central Library? Zip. Then I posted a query on a website, which led another historian, Chris Jepsen, to uncover this bit from the June 8, 1969 *Los Angeles Times*: "A shopping center… will be constructed on the northwest corner of Springdale and Warner Sts., Huntington Beach, with completion scheduled for late 1969…Designed by architect Lloyd Wright, son of the late Frank Lloyd Wright…Atlantic Richfield Co. will also build a service station, also designed by Wright, on a site at the apex of the center."

So this wasn't just a sign tower project? Wright was to have designed the entire center and gas station? I visited the site to investigate. I've passed it many times without noticing any details, but now what emerged (blunted by the store signage) were unique geometric shapes, angles and other nuances that seemed suspiciously…Wright-ous. Could it be?

Meanwhile, up near L.A., performance artist Patrick Tierney coincidentally did a web search on the shopping center. About twenty-five years ago, Tierney, an avid architecture student with a keen interest in Lloyd Wright, had found the tombstone too. Now, he checked occasionally to see if the landmark beguiled anyone else out in the universe. Stunned, he found my posting. He sent a response saying he had the story. Pay dirt.

Several days later, Tierney explained how a friend showed him the marker and how it set him off on a quest. After years, he tracked down the center's developer, Stanley Fann. Amazingly, Tierney was able to procure from Fann the architectural renderings of the Westfair center, as it was called. He treasures these plans, he said. After all, Frank Lloyd Wright Jr. designed them. It was true. Both the center and the Arco station were Wright's.

As for the tower, Tierney explained that locals vehemently protested the idea of a ninety-four-foot behemoth in their neighborhood, thwarting the plans of the great architect. The tombstone was placed, in Tierney's words, as "a 500-pound, permanent proclamation of victory of the People's will over art—a landmark stealing the same spot of earth where Wright's landmark would've stood." Tierney's assessment of Westfair is impressive. "There are several giveaway gestures that ring of [Wright's] influence. The center breezeway connecting the parking on both sides of the building.

"Then there's the telltale patterned staccato rows of 'Wright kite forms' (30-degree by 60-degree diamond forms) I call them, perching like gargoyle geo-solids on the roof edges, and serving as the center's leitmotif. Wright loved the 30-degree by 60-degree diamond shape because, he said, those angles are commonly found in nature." He adds that despite

A very rare image: Frank Lloyd Wright Jr.'s original artwork for the tower that never was.

Wright's original blueprints being somewhat compromised, the Arco station is "still a gem...the custom-fabricated steel wings over the pumps are similar to the cantilevers on many of his residential projects and I feel those could have been inspired by his work in the Los Angeles war plane factories during WWII."

Eventually, Tierney wants to write a long-form piece about the center and organize a walking tour at the site. Of course, he'll show off his original Wright rendering and a model of the original service station. When he does this, we should all be there. I also spoke with eighty-year-old Stanley Fann, who hired Wright. Now retired in Marina Del Rey, he confirms Tierney's facts, and then some. The tower controversy, as it turns out, was akin to a modern-day range war.

"Folks didn't want their community disturbed, so they fought back hard. Mr. Wright was just looking to create something grand and dramatic to help draw people to the center. And it had a heck of an unusual design." Fann adds that Wright also desired an ornate fountain, but it was too expensive. Though he planned on teaming up again with Wright to create another center (at Lakewood Boulevard and Carson Street in Bellflower), the project never materialized, making this the only Wright-designed shopping center.

Fann still has the original tower plans, so who knows? Perhaps someday it will find a rightful (and welcome) place here. And that tombstone? Fann says it illustrates the epic battle between residents and Wright, "Though I still wish the tower had survived," he said, chuckling.

Interviewing shop owners at Westfair hadn't seemed critical before because the tower seemed to be part of just the gas station. But veteran retailers here know the secret. Calvin Free at the venerable Beef Palace remembers his dad telling him of the tower controversy back in 1970 and that its design resembled something like a giant oil derrick. He also describes how city fire department recruits come looking for the tombstone as part of a routine scavenger hunt they're sent on to help familiarize themselves with the city. Matt Borgerson, who was twelve when the center opened, owns Crown Cleaners. He'd heard that at some point a Jerry Lewis Cinema was planned for the back parking lot. Today, he thinks people would love to know more about Westfair, with its "weird angles and shapes." Natalie Bryson, owner and manager of the West End clothing shop since 1970, knows about Wright's involvement but says nobody ever asks about it.

All three proprietors say they wish the tower had been built. So do I. And so does Eric Lloyd Wright, the architect's son. Eric, who has his own architectural firm in Malibu, apprenticed for eight years with his grandfather, Frank Lloyd Wright, as well as working with his father on Westfair. He told me he remembers the tower saga well and that the edifice was deemed too visually overwhelming by the most vocal locals. And despite the challenges of building in a marshy area, he recalls the positives of the final product: "When Westfair opened, it had a very good look to it, some very nice touches, as did the gas station."

Westfair may not have reached its own soaring potential. But it is Wright's. And it is ours. So let's bask in its odd history and let people know it's here. It's the least we can do to honor Frank Lloyd Wright Jr., who reached for the stars right here in Huntington Beach.

MEADOWLARK AIRPORT

How strange to be sitting at lunch at the site of the old Meadowlark Airport with the man whose name will be forever intertwined with it. For years I've read about Yukio "Dick" Nerio, who purchased the airport in 1947. But it was his son Art Nerio whom most old pilots identified with the venerable landing strip.

Though Art's parents lived on the property for a time, it was he who ran the airport through its most popular era in the 1960s through the late 1980s, when it closed. I've spoken to so many pilots who recount seeing Nerio pedal around on his bicycle collecting the three-dollar landing fees from planes as they taxied to a stop that I almost felt like I knew him already.

Now eighty-eight years old, Nerio still lives nearby, and I was very excited recently to be put in touch with him by his friend Linda Liem, who was a co-owner of the flight school that existed at the airport. As it happened, Mr. Nerio read my column recently on Meadowlark Airport, in which I talked about trying to track down the iconic blue sign that once sat out on Warner. As I wrote then, I had a few leads on the whereabouts of the sign, but Mr. Nerio wanted to set the record straight.

Over lunch, Nerio, Liem and her husband, Ron, and I talked about the airport. But we also learned about the Nerio family history. I did not realize that his family had been sent to an internment camp in Arkansas at the start of World War II. Art was a teenager then, and when his family was released, they returned to the area and thankfully all the property they owned in Orange County was still in their name. They lived where the Westminster Mall is located today, and before selling the property, Nerio told me you could see all the way up to the ocean from their backyard. (Art's dad was keen on buying up lots of property back then, which obviously served the family well.)

I learned about Brandy, the airport horse that belonged to Nerio's daughter, and the fact that he had a student pilot's license, which would not allow him to solo but still allowed him the flexibility of taking to the air with other licensed pilots.

His family still owns a good deal of property in the area, and to see the twinkle in his eye, he's always looking for more. Shrewd, tough and sturdy, Art Nerio was a fascinating person to have lunch with.

But it got better.

Afterward, Liem, her husband and I accompanied Mr. Nerio to his house. Once there, I had a

Art Nerio having lunch with the author in a restaurant located right on the site of the old Meadowlark Airport.

Art Nerio stands in his backyard, where he still has the original Meadowlark Airport sign.

chance to look over the many curios related to the airport, including civic plaques and scrapbooks bursting with old newspaper clippings and weathered photos. But the surprise treat was in the backyard, sitting up against a wall and covered with an old blue tarp. Ron, Linda and I peeled back the layers of blue plastic to reveal not just the Meadowlark Airport sign but also the sign for the Meadowlark Café. Nerio's wife (who passed away several years ago) had suggested they keep them, and so since the airport closed, they have rested here just several blocks from where they lived in the first place.

As an amateur historian who loves helping preserve pieces of the past, it was thrilling to be in the presence of these artifacts. The old Meadowlark Airport phone booth, still covered with stickers, is also in the backyard. After talking about them a bit, Mr. Nerio said that it would be okay this summer for my son and me to come over and help refurbish these items, which, while still in good shape, are beginning to suffer some wear and tear. After that, hopefully, we can figure out some way to display them for the public.

I'd like to thank Mr. Nerio for his kindness in showing me these things and also Linda Liem and her husband for helping to arrange this meeting. This was a very memorable day in Huntington Beach for me, spent with thoroughly lovely people. And the sign mystery is now solved.

THE GOLDEN BEAR

I've been out promoting my new book, *Led Zeppelin Crashed Here: The Rock and Roll Landmarks of North America*, and a Huntington Beach landmark keeps creeping into the conversations: the famed Golden Bear nightclub. At a book signing recently, someone told me that not only did he frequent the Bear, but he was also part of the 1986 demolition crew. Dropping his voice to a whisper, he confided, "A lot of the debris was dumped down by Dog Beach to help shore up the sea wall—I grab a brick or two whenever I surf down there, man."

While I was being interviewed on National Public Radio, the host told me he'd seen a number of shows at the Bear (including Patti Smith and Peter Gabriel) and that it was his favorite Southern California venue. Then, on a KOCE-TV show, I met audio engineer Robert Carvounas, who may just be the biggest Golden Bear fan of all. In fact, the Huntington Beach local has been hard at work on a book about Huntington Beach's famed musical landmark, and over a recent cup of coffee near the club's original site, he showed me a bunch of his artifacts—photos, tickets, posters, matchbooks, bricks and other memorabilia.

"I think it's the most interesting place in Huntington Beach history," he says.

He wasn't of age in the 1960s, so he couldn't see Janis Joplin or Jimi Hendrix perform at the Bear, but he did attend several shows in the '80s before it was demolished. Some background: The Golden Bear opened at 306 Pacific Coast Highway (just across from the pier) as a restaurant in the 1920s, designed by renowned Southern California architect Ernest Ridenour. Movie stars back then would motor down from Hollywood for dinner after a day at the beach. By the early 1960s, the space had morphed into a music club. The Doors, Dizzy Gillespie, the Byrds, the aforementioned Hendrix and Joplin plus many others played the Bear. Junior Wells cut a live album at the Bear. Peter Tork was a dishwasher there just before being cast as a Monkee.

Under new ownership in the 1970s, the Golden Bear continued to grow as a seminal performance space. Linda Ronstadt, Steve Martin, Blondie, the Ramones, Neil Young—dozens of major label acts visited Huntington Beach to play the Bear.

Guitarist Robin Trower played the last show there on January 26, 1986, and several months later, the club was demolished. Portions of the structure were preserved and incorporated into the façade of a new Golden Bear that

Robert Carvounas stands in front of the site where the Golden Bear used to be, posing with a photo of the classic club.

opened several years later, but that incarnation failed quickly, and the club quickly disappeared in the blur and rebuilding of downtown.

As Carvounas and I walked over to the site recently, he pointed out where the entrance would have been—where a hot dog place is today. Around the corner, the ticket booth from the second Golden Bear remains—the last trace of a legend. Or is it?

As Carvounas explains, collecting pieces of the Golden Bear is a hobby for more than a few people as a way of holding on to the memories. A planter outside a downtown home is made of Golden Bear bricks, as is another fan's fireplace. A small piece of the structure rests in a local flower garden, and Carvounas himself has one of the exterior signs. "Lots of people grabbed pieces of the place," he says. "Because of the memories. There's never been another place like it here."

Stu Harold, who works at the Pierside Gallery, remembers the Golden Bear well, so it's appropriate that where he sits today is just about where the stage would have rested. "This is like sacred ground," he laughs. "You name it and they played here. And the Bear had this wonderful underground feel to it."

Musician Mark Volman of the legendary Turtles played the Golden Bear many times, and he told me it was a special place for the band. "We had great fan support there, and the place was very professional. They paid market value to bands, and between the Coach House [in San Juan Capistrano] and clubs in L.A. like the Roxy, the Golden Bear filled an important void. For us, it was always a good gig," he said. Robert Carvounas believes, as I do, that the city could use a venue like the Golden Bear today.

TOWER ZERO

Whenever I travel, either to a big city or small town, I enjoy looking for traces of the past—maybe a faded advertisement painted large on a building side or obscure ruins—some forgotten remnant that creates an echo of the past. Though the seemingly heartless churn of urban development has an efficient way of vanquishing many pieces of history, you'd be surprised at how many survive. You just have to know where to look. In studying Huntington Beach, I've come across some relic traces that might make for an interesting local history tour this summer, perhaps on a lazy Sunday afternoon.

The first site comes courtesy of my friend John Andrews, who noticed an odd structure parked at South Coast Supply on Goldenwest Street near Garfield Avenue. John thought it might be the old airport tower from Meadowlark Airport. I drove past, took some photos and realized that while John's guess was a smart one, it was actually the lifeguard Tower Zero that was at one time located on the old pier! I spoke with Ron Brindle, who owns the property, and he explained that it's being kept there as a favor to a friend. If you happen to be driving past, it's certainly worth a glance.

Next is the old jailhouse behind the Longboard Restaurant and Pub on Main Street. Many have seen it, but I bet just as many have not. Built in about 1914, this imposing brick-and-mortar cell was where the rowdiest Huntington Beach offenders spent the night, essentially in isolation.

Next to it is a row of other old brick cells, which are used for more innocent practices today, acting as storage units. Located just off Main Street, these cells were strategically placed to handle the flow from the bars along the main drag leading to the pier. (The city's original police station was next to these cells.) Just a couple blocks away at Sixth Street and Walnut Avenue is the Helme House, one of the most historic homes in the city. A mule team moved it from eleven miles away in Santa Ana to this corner in 1903.

Tower Zero as it looked while being held in storage before being hauled away by a private owner.

Many of you probably know the house, but look closely on the outside and you'll see the old horse-latching rings that were discovered during street reconstruction in 1992. In the terrific International Surfing Museum on Olive Avenue is an interesting chunk of city history: the cornerstone from the original Huntington Beach pier.

The next piece of history may be my favorite because I like trains and I'm constantly trying to envision what it was like to have trolley train cars cruising up the coast and stopping at Pacific Coast Highway and Main Street, where the station used to be. If you head to Seventeenth Street and Pacific Coast Highway and go down to the sand, there you will find some of the original track that used to run up and down the coast. It's crumbling away in many places, but it is there, and a train aficionado I know verified that it is in fact what it appears to be. Also, near Jack in the Box at PCH and Warner Avenue, old seams in the road from the tracks appear to be running into the beach parking lot next to the fast-food restaurant. If you head down to investigate this, on the way, make sure to walk out on the bluff at the Bolsa Chica Wetlands. The bunch of palm trees there marks where the famed

Huntington Beach Gun Club used to sit (and some foundation ruins are left in the ground).

Right next to that site you'll also be able to see World War II artillery mounts, which were erected on this vantage point hill to patrol the waters for enemy invaders (Surf City was never attacked though).

Heading back for a moment to the area where the old tracks lie in the sand, if you continue toward Dog Beach, pay attention to the tons of rubble that help support the wall leading down from the bluffs. A lot of it is what's left of old Main Street in Huntington Beach.

There are other bits and pieces of historic ephemera too. Supposedly, the pelican sculptures at city hall used to exist at the Seacliff Shopping Center. And the ever-observant John Andrews told me that the Old Navy store at Five Points used to be a movie theater. In fact, he said if you ever go in there, check out the roof and you'll see where the screens were once located.

Do you know of other historic Huntington Beach remnants? Take some time to study what's left of the old city. You never know when it might be too late.

THE PITS

I did something this week I haven't done in ages: I signed a petition. For a variety of reasons, it's normally not something I do, but when I heard that there was a movement to remove all fire rings from Southern California beaches, I could not resist.

Have you heard? Southern California Air Quality Management District (AQMD) has proposed amendments to Rule 444 that would result in the removal of all Southern California beach fire rings. The issue cropped up several years ago and recently hit a fever pitch down in Newport when some locals who live on the beach decided they'd had enough of fire rings, that the smoke irritated them.

Huntington Beach mayor Connie Boardman sent a strongly worded letter to the organization last week that began, "I am writing in strong opposition to the amendment of Rule 444 to add beaches to the list of prohibited areas for open fire burning. Doing so will diminish the passive and affordable recreational opportunities for millions and greatly impact our local economy."

Mayor Boardman went on to make a number of salient points regarding the economy. She also addressed the emotional attachment many locals have to the fire rings (which have been here more than sixty years), and just as importantly, she talked about the fact that compared to Newport and other cities, the fire rings at Huntington Beach are located, in most cases, far enough away from homes so that the smoke typically does not play a major part in residents' lives.

In the *L.A. Times* last week, Sam Atwood, spokesman for the Southern California AQMD, said this: "It doesn't take a rocket scientist to know that smoke is unhealthy and contains many harmful pollutants—some of which can cause cancer. And it doesn't take a costly scientific study to tell you that dozens of these fires in close proximity create very unhealthy levels of smoke for anyone near them, and for residents downwind."

But Mr. Atwood, don't you think it would take *some* sort of study to back up your noticeably biased and stilted argument that the smoke levels are automatically considered to be unhealthy to the point of requiring a ban? What is your methodology? Do you factor in wind? Distance from homes? Vastness of beach? How can you treat all beachside cities as if they are the same? You don't think, before banning all fire rings in all Southern California cities, that you owe the public at least a trace of evidence that they are really causing any sort of measurable harm? And what of the economic losses?

Funny how that doesn't seem to come up in any of your organization's arguments.

I understand that the smoke may bother some and that there are very real medical issues that, should one get close to the fire, will be affected. So then why not just avoid them? Beach fires, for the most part, are a nighttime activity. So why would people even gather at the beach at night without intending to enjoy a fire? And we have lots of beach, plenty of it where there are no fire rings.

My hunch is first it will be the fire rings at the beach. Then the ones in backyards. Then it will be BBQs. Because this is how it starts and this is the sort of encroachment we're seeing all over the country today with bureaucrats deciding what is right for us, surgically trying to impede life's little pleasures and freedoms, one step at a time.

Me, I adore the wild smell of the roaring fires dotting the coast in the summer night when I drive down PCH, windows down and cool wind blowing. Co-mingled with the hot dogs, marshmallows and salt in the air, that sweet scent for me is one of life's great aromatic ecstasies (rivaled only by the one-two olfactory punch of cigars and beer in the old Yankee Stadium). So, yes, I like rich, pungent scents that evoke place—especially when that place is the beach. If you want to convince me those things are bad, prove it with facts. Not emotion.

And to be huddled around a fire like that with family and friends goes beyond just beach town ritual. It is like a sacred tribal gathering, primal and powerful. It is how our culture evolved. Cooking your food over fire. Huddling with those you love. Basking in the glow and warmth while an ocean thunders nearby. In an increasingly sterile world, one micromanaged and oppressed by growing government agency interference, coastal fire rings provide a refreshing, rugged dose of "leave us the hell alone."

Opponents of fire rings point out there are those who burn their garbage, chemically treated wood and other harmful items. They are right. People who do that are irresponsible, and efforts should be made to stop them. The city may need to invest in those efforts. But banning fire rings for the actions of a few fools is, in my view, foolish as well.

For those who don't care for the fire pits, I respect your point of view. But even though you don't like them, do you really want them banned? What happens when something *you* love is banned by these same officials? Are you really for banning things that you merely perceive as a nuisance or irritation? Again, where is the evidence to support the draconian measures we are being threatened with? Does that matter at all?

LONG LIVE THE PITS

Several months ago, AQMD chairman William Burke proclaimed that he was "100% positive" he would be able to ban all fire rings in Southern California. Clearly, he underestimated the power of a little place called Huntington Beach.

As we learned in a vote last Friday, the fire pits are staying right here where they belong. The fate of the pits in Newport and Corona Del Mar remains up in the air, but that's their problem, not ours. As now seems all but evident, this mess started down there not because of any real health issues but for the simple and despicable fact that certain wealthy beachfront owners want to control what types of people visit their beaches.

But all I know is, we won. Was it a bit bittersweet that the entire AQMD proposal wasn't thrown in the trash where it belongs? Perhaps. Nevertheless, it was a monumental victory.

And just look at what we did in the process! We began exposing what would appear to be one of the most unscrupulous government agencies in the state, if not the entire country. We turned this into a national story, so

The author stands by one of the many fire pits located in Huntington Beach. The summer of 2013 will long be remembered by many as the year the city rose up against the AQMD and won the battle of the bonfires.

now millions of people will associate the AQMD with this issue. We created pressure that forced William Burke to resign from the Coastal Commission. We exposed his and Mayor Dennis Yates's preposterous words comparing Newport bonfires to Vietnam carpet bombing (to date, neither man has apologized to veterans). We exposed the apparent academic fraud of board member Clark Parker. Perhaps most importantly, we came together as a city. People of every political persuasion and economic level worked together to get this done. It was glorious.

And, yes, we saved the fire pits. Throughout this process, several AQMD employees have reached out to me. They are ashamed of their leaders, and with good reason. This issue was embarrassing on many levels—for our region, for our state but especially for the AQMD. As one staffer expressed to me, quietly, after the meeting, "You have no idea how huge a victory this is. They planned on wiping all of the rings out, quickly and quietly. But your city stopped them, and you should be very proud."

As for the meeting itself, to quote Dickens, "It was the best of times and it was the worst of times." Hundreds of anti-ban supporters were there in force, along with many political leaders, including our own Mayor Connie Boardman, assemblyman Travis Allen, members of our city council and other mayors, assemblymen and even a senator. On the pro-ban side were the same glum five or so people who have attended every meeting.

I have not reported this before, but several weeks ago, an AQMD insider sent me a warning. Evidently, last week, the AQMD sent a photographer to Huntington Beach to photograph fire rings where illegal substances were being burned. They found not one. My source warned me they would still introduce pictures in the meeting to prove their point. And there they were, date stamped from last March, before this issue was barely on the radar. When I got to speak and advised their scientist of what my source told me and then asked who took the photos, he turned his back on me.

Chairman Burke was his usual strutting and arrogant self, but the person who stole the show, in my opinion, was board member Josie Gonzales. Her comments during deliberations had the entire packed room scratching their heads. In a rambling and unfocused address, she asked her executive director questions that even he didn't seem to understand. To many of us, it sounded as if she was hearing this issue for the very first time. When she made it clear she would be voting for the ban, and crowd members shook their heads, she chided them, belligerently, for not knowing what they were doing. It was embarrassing.

But perhaps I'm being too harsh on Ms. Gonzales. Maybe she has a tough time keeping track of things. After all, as it states in her AQMD bio, "Gonzales currently serves on 29 boards, committees and commissions." Twenty-nine! The AQMD includes that information without a trace of irony, as if it's a good thing. Another reminder of what happens when committee-addicted politicians have too much power.

Board member Judith Mitchell followed with a similarly uninformed speech. Other members didn't utter a word. And then it was left to board member/Orange County supervisor Shawn Nelson to finally bring some sense into the room. He and board member/Santa Ana mayor Miguel Pulido have been strong, clear and focused critics of the AQMD during this boondoggle, and Nelson on this day was brilliant. In the end, he, Pulido, Michael Antonovich, John Benoit, Ben Benoit and Jan Perry all voted against their own organization's recommendations. But it was one vote short.

Still, remember, their initial plan was to ban every single fire pit in Southern California. As it stands, Huntington Beach will lose just a handful under the new regulations, but several of us are working to have those properly moved to fit the new distance measures so that we won't lose one of them. Thank you to Travis Allen for staying on this issue in Sacramento.

For now, Huntington Beach is free and clear. I asked when the AQMD monitors will be moved from the AES parking lot and was told it will happen in short order. Trust me, I will check every day to make sure that happens. That's the point after all of this, I think. This is a bureaucracy that, while monitoring everything else, clearly needs to be monitored itself. And so that's what we'll do.

Like many cinema monsters, it's easy to imagine the AQMD rising from the slime to take another swipe at us, just when we think we have won. Then again, after the public and private beating they've taken over this, I'm not sure they'll be up for another Huntington Beach thrashing anytime in the near future. But since I know they are reading this right now, I'll say it here: AQMD, we are ready for you.

Fire pits will burn long and strong in Huntington Beach, hopefully forever, because of the passion and commitment of so many of you. Thank you, one and all. We did it. We beat them.

SURF CITY USA ®

"What's in a name?" wrote Shakespeare. If the playwright was residing in Huntington Beach today, a few lawyers would let him know, that's almost for sure—thanks to a battle over a slogan and a small T-shirt shop.

Maybe you're aware of the lawsuit being stoked like fire-pit embers on a midnight beach, a line in the sand drawn between our own Huntington Beach and an upstart from the north, Santa Cruz. Some background: In 2004, Doug Traub, president of the Huntington Beach Conference and Visitors Bureau, filed twelve trademark applications with the U.S. Patent and Trademark Office giving Huntington Beach exclusive rights to promote itself as Surf City USA. Traub's plan also included the creation of a boatload of Surf City USA–branded goods and services, like clothing, bicycles, financial services and volleyballs. At the time, Traub said, "This is quite a moment for us when you consider the amount of research we have done with thousands of people and the subsequent efforts we have taken over the past few years to bring the Surf City USA brand to market. Our investment has helped us create a monumental lifestyle brand that complements and solidifies our emerging status as the premier overnight beach destination on the West Coast."

Both Huntington Beach and Santa Cruz had referred to themselves as Surf City for years, and though they had sparred good-naturedly over the conflict, the addition of USA to Huntington Beach's slogan forced a showdown last September. That's when Noland's on the Wharf, a forty-five-year-old beachwear shop on the Santa Cruz pier, received a letter from a Southern California law firm threatening to sue the family business. It accused Noland's of violating a trademark because for the last year it had sold a T-shirt featuring the words "Surf City, Santa Cruz, California, USA." Bruce Noland (whose parents founded the store) was caught off guard, saying he was unaware that Huntington Beach had even applied for a trademark, let alone owned one. With controversy stirring, the remaining shirts became hot items, fetching as much as $1,000 apiece on eBay.

Ginger Noland, the family matriarch, told the Santa Cruz tourist board about the legal threat, and the laid-back college town rallied behind Noland's. Then a local law firm offered up pro bono service to battle Huntington Beach. A trial is set for Northern California in September 2008, with Santa Cruz suing Huntington Beach under the claim that the trademark of Surf City USA is not enforceable beyond the general Huntington Beach area. So much for good vibrations. (Interestingly, two places in the United States are actually named "Surf City" in New Jersey and North Carolina; the latter features the slogan "Big enough to be competitive, but small enough to be happy!" Where they fit into this eddy one can only imagine.)

I asked Traub about the lawsuit, and he was adamant: "What folks have to be aware of is that the bureau's trademark was attacked by Santa Cruz merchants who violated our trademark rights. We believe when this matter goes to court, they will lose. The only real question is whether our countersuit will allow us to collect meaningful damages for their actions; we are asking for a damage award in excess of $1 million." He also clarified an important point: "The issue is about a trademark for Surf City USA and not over use of the term 'Surf City,' which anyone is free to use." (Good news for Surf City Tanning, Surf City Nails, Surf City Escrow, Surf City Coin Laundry and about seventy other local businesses.)

Up in Santa Cruz, Bruce Noland told me he was genuinely unaware that his shirts violated anything. Seeing how the words are stacked in the design, with USA isolated from Surf City, it seems innocent. Noland explains that none of this court fight would be possible without pro bono legal assistance, and he worries about what happens if he and his mom are forced to pay a $1 million fine. It appears he landed in the middle of a firestorm coincidentally, and he's dealing with it as best he can. Would he be happy with just "Surf City"?

He thinks so. But this confrontation has reached another level, perhaps past the point of no return. "People here felt we were getting bullied," he said. "I guess that's why so many wanted to fight back." I see both sides of this: the global "destination marketing" drive of Huntington Beach and the small-town fighting spirit up in those bohemian redwoods.

That said, nothing drains the laid-back charm out of a slogan like Surf City USA faster than nasty courtroom combat. Traub said, "The Surf City USA brand is about the lifestyle and spirit of Southern California, of which Huntington Beach is the perfect example. We are redefining what California beach towns are all about, while staying true to our roots with an authenticity that appeals to all demographics and age groups." This sounds less about surfing and more about overall lifestyle. Santa Cruz, on the other hand, seems more focused on promoting a pure surfing culture. So I suggest this: let Huntington Beach own Surf City USA®. Let Santa Cruz own Surfing City USA®. And let peace prevail®.

OLD PIRATE LANE

I wish every street in Huntington Beach had a Gwendoline Runyard. She passed away in January 2013 at ninety, a year after her husband John, but left behind a remarkable trove of memories inspired by the neighborhood where she lived.

Runyard wrote in 1955: "During my search for a larger house for a larger family I found Old Pirate Lane. Here stood one old country type red farm house, with matching barn, positioned on this rarely traveled grass, gravel, and dirt track which led to the edge of a little airport. The house faced Graham Street." The farmhouse, built in 1906 by the Graham family (and no longer red), still stands. As does the house the Runyard family built in the '50s and pretty much every other house originally constructed on this dead-end side street that doesn't run much beyond the length of a football field.

Old Pirate Lane as it looked in the 1960s.

But what a wonderful little world it represents—a peek back to simpler, uncluttered, more rugged Huntington Beach.

Runyard, a poet and family archivist, published a small book some years ago named for her street. Her son John and I used it as a guide as we walked the neighborhood of his youth. The small paperback details the stories behind every house and each family who lived in those houses, in both words and rare pictures.

John painted a fine picture for me, recalling the lush, thick, fragrant orange and eucalyptus groves, the agriculture—and the horses. His family, along with several others, kept horses in their backyards (along with goats, bunnies, chickens, pigs and even a burro). In the early '60s, John and his brothers would ride their horses to the beach, trotting down Warner before cutting across the wetlands and moseying to the sea. Can you imagine that today?

In the Runyard backyard are remnants of the rich past: the hay shed for the horses, citrus trees and an old swing set visible in some of his Mrs. Runyard's vintage photos. A sign, "The Runyard Ranch," hangs from a shingle. Just how quaint was life here in the early '60s? One day, the two Runyard horses jumped the fence. They were found soon after, grazing at Meadowlark Golf Course.

The golf course factored in when the kids wanted to make money too. Before the high nets or fences were put in place to catch errant balls, Runyard and his pals would retrieve the shanked shots and sell them back to the golfers for a quarter apiece.

Then there was the sand pit, located just down Graham, right before you hit Warner. This was a sixty-foot-high, steep crested ridge that led down to a fresh pool of water where local kids would make rafts and hunt for crawfish. That is, when they weren't riding horses or tending to other farm animals.

Seventy-three-year-old Ralph Ricks soon joined us on our stroll. He moved to Old Pirate Lane in 1973 (his house, located at the end of the street, was moved here from Belmont Shore in the mid-'60s). His yard spilled into Meadowlark Airport, and after enough pilots bummed water and electricity from him, he decided to buy a plane, and then the pilots gave him flying lessons. He parked his craft in his front yard.

He and John recalled the old pepper tree, a constant fixture in Gwendoline Runyard's writings. Once located in the middle of the street, the neighborhood focal point was torn down a number of years ago to make room for a new house. Just like the old oak tree was. Sure, a few things have changed, and from time to time, the pot gets stirred. Like when, as Ricks described, a "Newport lawyer moved in and started complaining about the roosters."

Ricks also explained why the street is now called Old Pirate Drive (versus Lane). See, the federal government, in its infinite wisdom, decreed that lanes would now run only north and south, and drives would run east and west, like Old Pirate. If one of the bureaucrats who made this decision ever had a moment to visit, he might understand just how foolish the blanket law was. After all, Old Pirate is not a "drive." It is most certainly a "lane."

Oh, and I can't forget the famed, faded pink tank that provides water just for this neighborhood. "The Old Pirate Water Company," Ricks laughed. "No chlorine, just the best-tasting water in the city. Our own private well." All the neighbors share repairs and upkeep equally, of course, and some of the handier residents get in and fix it themselves when it gets stubborn.

There is a palpable peace in the air back here; a gentle, country quality that first lured Gwendoline Runyard here to stake her family's claim. It is a special place.

Ricks disappeared from our conversation, and soon, he was rumbling down the lane in his bright yellow 1911 Ford Model T. It was the perfect touch as it passed the farmhouse that was built just five years before the car.

I thought it appropriate that we close with one of Mrs. Runyard's poems, entitled "OPL—Then and Now."

Dappled shade of the pepper tree
Half-way down the Lane,
Was welcome in the Summer's sun
'til sea winds blew cool again.
Eucalyptus trees in rows
Line some boundaries in the sun.
Grass struggles through the gravel path
In the road not yet begun.
Quiet. lies in the meadows here
Far from cities busy roar,
Enjoying the gift of the Spring rains,
Oblivious of what's in store.
For some day soon, the road will burst
With builders' trucks, and cranes,
Yet despite the construction's noise,
This rustic lane remains

THE RED CARS

I will never forget several years ago, when a friend directed me down to the beach adjacent to about Ninth Street to discover a vital piece of Huntington Beach history. There, embedded in the ground, are remnants of the old train tracks that supported the Pacific Electric Red Cars that started running here more than one hundred years ago.

My son Charles, a USC sophomore who is working on his first history book, had an idea recently based on the Red Car trains. He said, "Dad, a lot of people are familiar with the trolley that ran up and down the coast because of how prominent it was and also because of the many photographs. But there were other train lines through Huntington Beach. How about a column that traces the other routes?"

Great idea, son! And so with his research, I will talk about them in this column.

Some background: As you may know, railroad magnate Henry Huntington ran his trains down here, and in exchange, "Pacific City" became "Huntington Beach." Huntington was smart. He was less concerned about mass transportation and more concerned with making it easy for people to visit places he was developing so that he could increase real estate sales. In the 1940s, Los Angeles actually had more than nine hundred Red Cars that covered more than 1,100 miles all throughout the Southland. (The last Red Cars in Southern California ran in 1961.)

Here in Huntington Beach, we had a big depot located right at PCH and Main. That was there until the early 1950s, at which point it moved over to Atlanta for several years and then was torn down.

But if we were back in the 1940s, just where could you hop on one of the trains in and around Huntington Beach?

Here's how it broke out. Starting in Seal Beach, along the Newport/ Balboa line, was the East Side station stop near Seal Beach Boulevard. Then came the Pensla stop, the Bridgeport stop and the Surfside Colony stop across from what used to be Sam's Seafood.

Continuing south was the Bayview stop, Twenty-third Street, Sunset Beach near Sixteenth and Pacific, the Ninth Street stop and a Fifth Street stop. In the traffic circle, where today Warner dead-ends at PCH near Jack in the Box, was the Los Patos stop.

A red car train in Huntington Beach, circa 1915.

Now you are in Huntington Beach. There was a Bolsa Chica stop either at the old gun club or where the current beach pay station is; we are not quite sure. Just south of Sea Point was the Stolco stop and then the Rocamp stop near Dog Beach.

There were station stops at Twenty-third Street, Seventeenth Street, Twelfth Street, Eighth Street, Fifth Street and of course Main Street.

Beyond that the train stopped at First Street, at the trailer park, Gamewell (PCH and Beach Boulevard) and the Pacific Gun Club. Finishing up in HB along the coast were stops at "Nago" (at Magnolia and PCH) and finally at Melrose (located at Brookhurst). The trains then continued to Newport Beach.

There were two other lines in Huntington Beach that supported the Red Cars. The La Bolsa line started at First Street and PCH and featured four other stops: Westfall (Adams between Lake and Alabama), Newland (Yorktown between Ranch and Huntington), Holly Sugar Plant (Garfield and Main) and Weibling (Ellis between Gothard and Huntington).

Finally, the Santa Ana/Huntington Beach, which also started at First and PCH, traveled diagonally to Beach Boulevard and Indianapolis, wended east along Indianapolis to Bushard and then north along Bushard to Talbert before heading east to Costa Mesa (with too many HB stops to name in this space!).

So now you know at least the partial extent of Red Car traffic in Huntington Beach.

In addition to the track remnants you'll find on the beach, there are a couple other telltale Red Car traces. One is a train crossing sign that once stood somewhere in the city of Huntington Beach. I noticed it at an old supply lot not long ago and actually purchased it. It's a bit cumbersome, and I'm still waiting for somebody with a truck to help me get it into my house.

Also, a stretch of right of ways, as they were called—the actual paths the trains ran—still can be seen from the La Bolsa line. The tracks may be gone, but narrow grass medians represent where the trains once creaked along. I photographed a portion of one for this column, from where the Westfall stop was on Adams near Lake.

To enjoy more Red Car history today, you can visit the Red Car Museum in Seal Beach or actually ride an old Red Car in San Pedro, where they still maintain a 1.5-mile vintage trolley line.

THE GOODYEAR BLIMP

When the Goodyear Blimp takes off, you're looking almost straight up into the sky. On the way down, it's the same thing in reverse—and the ground comes at you fast. Beyond those two extremes, though, the ride itself is a soothing, gentle cruise that seems to slow down the hectic pace of life. Through your headset, your pilot points out various sites along the coast near Long Beach, but truth be told, the mind wanders at one thousand feet, taking in the slow-motion ride foot by foot.

So I learned several months ago. I was writing a story for *Westways Magazine* on the fortieth anniversary of the blimp being at the Carson Air Station, so I was fortunate enough to be invited along for a ride one warm, breezy day in May. I learned a lot about the hallowed ship during my research and, of course, on my journey aboard. But I also became aware that the man I was profiling for the *Westways* piece, Bob Urhausen, is a Huntington Beach local. Since the blimp first arrived in January 1968, Urhausen has been working there. Except for a two-year stint in the U.S. Army (he was

The Goodyear blimp as it prepares to dock in Carson, California. The author and his family were lucky enough to ride aboard the ship courtesy of Bob Urhausen.

honorably discharged in 1971), Bob has worked at the air base in a variety of positions, including crewman, airship rigger and, since 1979, as the public relations manager for the Goodyear Airship in Carson. His knowledge of the famed craft is exceeded perhaps only by his enthusiasm for the ship, and he seems just as awed by the blimp today as he presumably was back when he was a college student. But he also loves Huntington Beach.

"My wife and I moved to Huntington Beach from Hermosa Beach in 1980," he told me. "There is just something about salt air that keeps me near the beach." Urhausen, born in Santa Cruz, moved to Redondo Beach with his family at age five. After ending his time in the army in 1971, he lived in Hermosa Beach until 1980. He and his wife, Barb, have been married for twenty-eight years. "She and I met while the blimp was on 'summer tour' up the Northwest [Portland], although she is from Mankato, Minnesota," Urhausen said.

Urhausen's two children graduated from Marina High School. His son, Eric, almost twenty-seven, will soon graduate from the Art Institute. His daughter, Nicole, twenty-three, is a 2007 graduate of Cal State Long Beach and is now earning her teaching credential. Bob is a funny, genial man who so genuinely enjoys what he does that it's infectious—you love the blimp even more after hearing Bob wax on about it. From time to time I notice it over our house, and so I wondered if Bob ever flew over Surf City.

"I have flown over Huntington a few times; however, my job keeps me on the ground a lot, so it is a special treat when I fly," he said. "The blimp, on the other hand, gets over Huntington Beach quite often. One of our former pilots, Tom Matus—now retired but still living in Huntington Beach—would fly over every chance he could. Recently, one of our new pilots, Kristen Davis, bought a home in Huntington Beach, and she gets out there often."

And as I said, he loves this town like he loves the ship. "From the time I first surfed Huntington Beach back in the '60s, I loved the access to the beach," he said. "Even today on my way home from work, I will take the long way just to drive down Warner to Pacific Coast Highway and follow PCH to the pier just to see the majestic beauty that is Huntington Beach. Huntington Beach has been a great place to live and raise a family. As I travel the country with the Goodyear blimp, I am always proud to tell people that I live in Huntington Beach, California."

Bob says he is often asked how folks can get a ride in the blimp. "Much as we'd love to give all Goodyear tire buyers a ride, it's reserved primarily for corporate customers," he says. "We donate rides to charities and fundraisers, and they've been known to raise as much as $5,000 to $8,000 at auction for two seats on board." Some more blimp facts: Its skin is as thick as a trampoline, a two-ply polyester fabric that's very strong and very hard to tear. Also, blimps can last about seven to eight years. And the daily flight schedule involves five one-hour passenger flights each day if the ship is not away covering a game or other event. Then there's a sixth, non-passenger flight, in the evening. It's a promotional flight around the area with the message-board lights on. (At Goodyear's other two air bases, in Akron, Ohio, and Pompano Beach, Florida, the same basic schedule is maintained.)

So next time you see the Goodyear Blimp overhead, know that our own Bob Urhausen, perhaps her biggest fan, may be onboard. But even if he's not, his heart is always up there with her.

Mysterious Phone Poles

Houston, we have a problem. Or at least, we had a problem. That was until a little mystery involving outer space, the Apollo program and telephone poles was solved earlier this week.

A couple months ago, my friend Huntington Beach marine safety chief Kyle Lindo wrote me with a suggestion for a column after seeing this on the official Huntington Beach website:

"Huntington Beach contains a major installment of one of the state's largest employers, Boeing, formerly McDonnell Douglas. A number of installments on the Boeing campus were originally constructed to service the Apollo Program, most notably the production of the S-IVB upper stage for the Saturn IB and Saturn V rockets, and some nearby telephone poles are still marked 'Apollo Dedicated Mission Control Line.'"

Lindo wondered, as I did after reading, if these poles still existed and just what exactly they were. Presumably some sort of direct, private contact to Mission Control from Huntington Beach, but it sounded interesting.

So I started researching or, shall I say, driving around Huntington Beach, in the Boeing neighborhood primarily, looking at telephone poles. Lots of telephone poles. But nothing.

Oddly, searching for information online revealed nothing—except that the original passage has been copied and pasted numerous times into many other sites that talk about Huntington Beach history, with no further explanation.

I e-mailed a group of locals with a general question about any information leading to these telephone poles. I received many responses, most to the effect of, "We know nothing about these but please let us know what you discover."

My friend Chris Jepsen, an archivist at the Orange County Archives and terrific local expert, wrote, "I've heard that line about the telephone poles, but I've never been able to verify it. Very cool if true, but who knows?"

And I received this from Janis Mantini, a former Boeing employee: "Chris, we looked all over campus for poles with these markings and we were never able to find them. We think it might be an urban legend. We heard this story [at] the end of the year 2011 and our facilities guys were all over looking for them but none were located."

OK. Finally. At least a potential bit of information. But information that may suggest they never even existed!

In the interim, as I researched, poked and prodded, I thought I might reach out to an old high school classmate—one who, if asked, "What are you, a rocket scientist?" can actually answer, "Yes." Jim O'Kane is a real-life rocket scientist and the general manager of Seahorse Systems, LLC. He's also extremely good at making complex things seems simple. So I asked him about these telephone poles.

O'Kane explained that Douglas Aircraft was the prime contractor for the third stage of the Saturn V during the Apollo missions and that the people at the Huntington Beach office knew everything about the construction and operation of their part of the vehicle. He added that the experts here needed to be available in real time for any emergency or problem that came up during the quarter-million-mile trip to the moon.

He went on to explain that long before we had satellite phones and fiberoptic cables, there were only hard-wired copper phone and data lines connecting business offices to Western Electric phone switches. NASA built into all its prime contractors' agreements a requirement that the primary designers would need to provide 24/7 availability for Mission Control staff in Houston to talk instantly to various "back rooms" full of hardware engineers across the country. Those hard-wired lines were vital to analyze mission data immediately during a flight.

O'Kane added, "Noting this on telephone poles was no doubt a great marketing idea for Douglas. I think an example of getting in touch with the back room at Douglas was during the Apollo 6 mission, an unmanned test of the Saturn V that was trouble-plagued through the entire launch. I'm sure those dedicated phone lines were humming as the launch vehicle did almost everything it could to tear itself apart during liftoff. There were probably a lot of strongly worded engineers' opinions zipping over those lines that day."

Interestingly, O'Kane said that making a phone call back then would have taken ten to twelve seconds to connect, so these dedicated lines existed so that there would be no delay in getting answers. Sort of like the audio equivalent of closed-circuit television. These lines were separate from the normal switched lines of the regular Bell System so as not to interrupt any local service.

OK, so now, even if I never saw one of these poles, at least I knew what they had been used for.

As I was putting this story to bed last week, I received this e-mail from Jill Hardy, a teacher at Marina High School who had received my original outreach: "Chris, I asked my Marina students if they had seen one of these signs. Today one came to me and told me he found one. It is at Edwards and McFadden in front of the Mormon Church."

My son and I went to the site at once. And sure enough, there it was. On the telephone pole, an artifact from the Apollo era. Yellow letters on black bands of metal affixed to the pole: "Apollo Bolsa Team."

The student who noticed this is a freshman named Michael Bonomo. I called first to thank him and then ask him how it caught his eye. He told me as his grandmother drove him to school one day, they were stopped at the red light and his eyes drifted up. Remembering Hardy's challenge from almost two months earlier, he realized he had made contact.

I drove along McFadden in search of others, but it seems that this is the only one. That's OK. At least we have one, a connection to the vaunted Apollo program developed in part right here in Huntington Beach—and a mystery positively solved thanks to the eagle eye of an adept high school student. Thank you, Michael, and everyone else who became part of this adventure.

GUN CLUB

What do Teddy Roosevelt, King Gustaf of Sweden, the Prince of Wales and Pope Pius XII all have in common, as it relates to Huntington Beach? They all visited the Bolsa Chica Gun Club.

Opened around 1900 on property that is now the Bolsa Chica wetlands, the club boasted a beautiful redwood and cedar hunting lodge and many amenities catering to the well-heeled duck hunters of the day. Initially, membership in the club was limited to forty, with an initial membership fee of $1,000 and annual dues of $60, making it one of the most exclusive clubs in the area.

I've learned much of what I know about the club from my friend David Carlberg, renowned microbiologist, environmental activist and author of several books, including the exceptional *Bolsa Chica: Its History from Prehistoric Time to the Present*.

David, along with his wife, Margaret, has long been active in the Amigos de Bolsa Chica. But he also has a keen interest in the history of the gun club, which is why I arranged for us to actually walk the site of the club's ruins. Neither of us had ever had the opportunity to have access across the fence, so recently he, my son and I were led on a walking tour by Taylor Vanberkum from Fish & Game.

And what a fascinating experience it was. I have often walked the trail near the original site of the club, looking through the fence and wondering what it might be like to actually explore the area. On the warm, sunny day we were there, dry winds blew the high grasses, creating a heavy "whisper" that all but drowned the nearby ocean waves.

I could not believe Dave had never been back here before, given his extensive research and analysis of the Bolsa Chica Gun Club's history. But here we were, examining the old foundation and road that led to the club and lining up old photos to notice that many of the original palm trees were still in place, swaying over knotty groves and thick wild mustard plants rather than a members' clubhouse.

My mind flashed back to the 1930 film *Sara and Son* starring Frederic March that featured several key scenes shot right here at the site—some of the only known film footage of the structures that were once here. But all was not Hollywood and male bonding over brandy at the end of a long day. Tensions arose out here when, in order to create bigger duck ponds, the club members blocked the natural tidal flow, infuriating the many peat land ranchers and farmers.

Carlberg also explained to us how, after the military was done using the site post–World War II (that area of the bluff had gun mounts then to protect us from a potential seaside attack), the land was given back to the club. But its best days had passed, and soon after, it closed.

Then, according to Carlberg, it was either torn down or it burned down in the late 1960s, leaving little today except some concrete foundations, what appears to be a rusted hay wagon and a lot of errant, rusted piping and rubble. Nature had done a predictably good job reclaiming the site.

Interestingly, we noticed lots of seashell fragments, which Carlberg told us probably dated back to when a Native American Holocene coastal

The Bolsa Chica Gun Club can be seen in this 1933 photo as men survey damages from the Long Beach Earthquake, which had happened just days before.

village existed here some eight thousand years ago. On the very interesting historicwintersburg.blogspot.com website, there is more information relating to the club.

Reading there, I learned about the Okuda family, for whom the Bolsa Chica Gun Club was home for over two decades. As it states, "Harry Okuda maintained the landscaping and kitchen gardens, including the yard of chickens being readied for club members' dinners. Harry arrived at the Gun Club circa 1910 or 1913—coinciding with his arrival in the United States" (from Japan). Seventy-five years later, in 2005, Carlberg sat down with then eighty-four-year-old Jimmie Okuda, Harry's son, to learn about his life at the club. Carlberg wrote about Okuda in the Amigos de Bolsa Chica's summer 2005 newsletter, *Tern Tide*. When not attending school in Huntington Beach, Okuda told Carlberg, he spent his days "fishing and swimming in the lagoon, helping tend his mother's chickens or enjoying sunsets from the beach."

It was impossible not to think about the Okuda family as we stepped carefully through the overgrown brush surrounding the former gun club site.

But that is the magic of wandering in a place that holds so much history—the stories seem to hang in the air, alive in the breeze, trapped in the very trees that bore witness to it all so many years ago.

Here, where prominent local men with names like Torrance, Slauson and Huntington roamed, where the Okuda family came of age and where even Teddy Roosevelt left his footprints (and, no doubt, a few less ducks). Right here in Huntington Beach.

THE CULT

This year marks the fortieth anniversary of a strange chapter in Huntington Beach history. The effects of this chapter are still felt today all over the world, and firestorms of controversy have burned all along the way.

Let me frame this story. Several weeks ago, I watched a riveting British documentary that aired on MSNBC. It was called *Cult Killer: The Ricky Rodriguez Story.*

The background on the documentary is: Two decades after a Christian religious sect officially renounced adult-child sex in response to allegations of sexual misconduct, *Cult Killer* was produced to revive many of the questions. The sect, known as the Family International and commonly known as the Family, was founded in the late 1960s with thousands of members worldwide. In January 2005, Ricky Rodriguez, the onetime heir apparent to the Family, fatally stabbed his former nanny and then shot himself dead.

He left chilling videotape alleging that the sexual abuse he had suffered as a child at the hands of members of the group was the reason he was about to exact revenge. The tapes he shot of himself describing his unbelievably depraved upbringing formed the centerpiece of the documentary. They were dramatic, compelling and deeply disturbing.

The Family, which was actually first called the Children of God when formed by David Berg, was among the movements prompting the cult controversy of the 1970s and 1980s in the United States and Europe and triggered the first organized anti-cult group, Free the Children of God.

Among the Family's thousands of members is Jeremy Spencer, the former Fleetwood Mac guitarist. How he wound up in the sect stands as one of rock-and-roll's more bizarre stories.

In 1971, Spencer went to buy some newspapers one day at a bookstore on Hollywood Boulevard (Fleetwood Mac had just kicked off a tour of America). But he never came back. He'd been approached by a member of the Children of God and, almost instantly, fell under their spell.

When the guitarist failed to show up for that evening's gig, the police were contacted, and after five worry-filled days, Spencer was traced to the Children of God headquarters at a warehouse in downtown Los Angeles. In order to get in to see Spencer, Fleetwood Mac manager Clifford Davis had to make up a story about Spencer's wife, Fiona, being seriously ill. According to a Fleetwood Mac roadie who was at the scene, Spencer "was walking around in a daze like a zombie…he'd been brainwashed. It nearly killed me to see him." His head had been shaved, and he now answered to the biblical name Jonathan.

After a three-hour talk, during which members of the cult rubbed Jeremy's arms and chanted, "Jesus loves you," Spencer explained he had tired of the hedonistic rock-and-roll lifestyle and that he was through with the group.

Today, it is believed Spencer is still involved with the Children of God. There are other celebrity connections. Actor River Phoenix spent his early childhood in the Family. His parents had joined in 1972, and Phoenix and his siblings often sang and performed on street corners for food. Eventually, Phoenix's parents grew disillusioned with the Children of God and left in 1977. Actress Rose McGowan was also raised in the Family.

But it was Ricky Rodriguez's story that had me on the edge of the couch, watching in both amazement and disgust as he detailed the abuse he was forced to endure and take part in. The adopted son of Berg, he was to have carried on the faith; he was the chosen one. But he escaped the madness, and the rest is brutal history.

Getting back to the start of this column, just what is the strange anniversary in Huntington Beach history? Well, it was here, in 1968, that Berg started the Family. Berg, a former Christian and Missionary Alliance minister, started operating an independent Christian ministry in Huntington Beach in 1967. His mother lived here, which is one reason he arrived. Another reason was the throngs of impressionable young people looking for a new way. Called the Teen Challenge, Berg's group was a youth ministry of the Assemblies of God. He separated the group from the national Teen Challenge organization, renamed it Light Club and ran it from a Main Street coffee house where he preached. It was here that Berg found his life's calling and the movement now known as the Family had its birth. (Berg would die in 1994.)

The Family gave this nation (and other parts of the world) some first tastes of the concept of a modern-day "cult," and many of the charges it faced over the years (and what Ricky Rodriguez painfully documents on video) are far too lurid to be documented in these pages. I recommend Don Lattin's excellent book, *Jesus Freaks: A True Story of Murder and Madness on the Evangelical*

Edge, if you're interested in a full-blown, well-documented history of the Family. But be warned—it is not for the faint of heart.

The next time you're walking downtown, perhaps you'll pause for a moment outside 116 Main Street. Today it's a retail shop, but forty years ago, during a psychedelic summer, it became ground zero for one of the most controversial movements in American history.

THE CHURCH AT WINTERSBURG

"Jesus Lives" reads the rainbow-themed mural painted on the side of the old church building at Warner Avenue and Nichols Lane. Inside, another painting: on a large wall of the church, "I Love Taylor Walsh" has been spray painted in day-glo pink by some recent uninvited visitors.

Such is the confused state of the historic former Wintersburg Japanese Presbyterian Church, which dates back to 1934.

I had the special privilege recently of taking an insider's tour of the compound along with a host of other local historian types and interested

The old church at Warner Avenue and Nichols Lane.

parties, courtesy of Rainbow Environmental Services. They own the property and led the tour as a means of creating some dialogue that may help determine the fate of the church and the rest of the farm property (which includes the family house and several other historic structures).

The group included Reverend Ted Esaki from the Wintersburg Presbyterian Church, Dann Gibb from Fountain Valley Historical Society, Art Hansen from CSU–Fullerton and Mary Adams Urashima, a government and public affairs consultant, among others.

Just how important is this site in terms of local history? Local historian Chris Jepsen put it well when he wrote recently, "This is the most important extant Asian American historical site in Orange County, and still features the Wintersburg Japanese Presbyterian Church—including the 1910 mission and manse, and the 1934 church—as well as the pioneer Furuta family's charming California bungalow."

If you ever look at a (really) old map of the area, you'll see the area was called Wintersburg. It was founded in the 1880s by a farmer named Henry Winters, and living here were some true pioneers of the county. There were the Gothards, Nichols and Graham, and a substantial Japanese community, including the Furuta family, who donated an acre of their property to build the original Wintersburg mission in 1910 (the church moved to Santa Ana in 1965 and now goes by the Wintersburg Presbyterian Church).

Since the early 1990s, the property has sat empty, removed from view the last several years by a tarp-wrapped fence. As we'd see soon, though, vandals and squatters have had their way with the place and certainly have altered what may or may not be salvageable.

The day of our tour, Jerry Moffatt, co-president/chief operating officer of Rainbow, briefed us beforehand. Not knowing yet the exact status of how they might develop property, he explained, clearly to the relief of those gathered, that the company would be willing to donate any costs associated with demolition toward moving some of the structures to keep them intact.

While that would not cover all the costs associated with moving, it is a generous, productive offer. After some other information about how to safely wander the grounds, we crossed the street and, as if entering some sort of time travel portal, were transported back to Huntington Beach, circa 1910.

The crops were gone, but wide-open spaces remained. The sounds of traffic faded away on the protected property, and the simple, honest, hard work of the immigrant Furuta family hung in the air.

Mary Urashima, who helped organize the tour, shared her impression: "It definitely was a step back into a quieter time. Warner Avenue was a dirt road;

most of the surrounding area would have been fields of celery or peppers. The home, mission and church were surrounded by lawns, goldfish ponds and garden. I got the impression that while those in Wintersburg obviously worked hard, there was a simple quality of life we don't experience today."

She's right. And even though the ponds, gardens and vegetables are no longer there, in the lazy, rural open space, they are easy to imagine.

The buildings we entered, including the 1910 and 1934 churches and the manse, were all soggy and heaving. Inside the structures, floors were collapsed, garbage was strewn everywhere and gang graffiti (along with the aforementioned pledge to Ms. Walsh) covered many walls.

But bits of the past remained.

In the 1934 church, brochures and hymnals from decades ago were scattered about, along with other interesting artifacts. It was fascinating to tiptoe through these sacred buildings, all of us whispering as if not to wake the spirits.

Back out in the daylight, the discussions all centered on what might be possible in terms of saving these vital structures. Some buildings seem more moveable than others.

But none of it seems easy. Or cheap.

As far as the future, Art Hansen, emeritus professor of history and Asian American studies at Cal State–Fullerton and former senior historian at the Japanese American National Museum in Los Angeles, offered this: "What I hope for next is that a realistic appraisal is made by certified historical preservationists of the costs involved in the total historical preservation of the structures on the Rainbow Disposal–owned site and that possible secure sites for their relocation and rehabbing and maintenance and interpretation be explored for their appropriateness and feasibility, financially and otherwise."

Urashima gave me her opinion was well: "It would be ideal if these historic buildings could remain in place. However, there needs to be an organization that can do the restoration, provide maintenance, security and manage visitors. Relocation to a site where this type of support system is already in place may be the best bet. I imagine some structures—such as the barn—would have to be disassembled to be moved. I would love to see the buildings go together to a museum or exhibition-type site where they can be visited and offer educational experiences about Orange County's agricultural development, the history of Wintersburg and Huntington Beach and the story of Japanese Americans in California."

So the good news is, this issue is very much alive. Yes, there are serious challenges, logistical and financial among them, but Rainbow Environmental

Services seems very amenable to doing what they can to help preserve this history, and that's a good thing.

Whatever happens, it might be worth slowing down or even pulling over near the intersection of Warner and Nichols just to absorb some of the rich history on the other side of the fencing. You can see a glimpse from the street of what's inside—a peek into a past that hopefully will have a future.

HE LOVES TAYLOR WALSH

Several weeks ago, I wrote about my tour of the former Wintersburg Japanese Presbyterian Church at Warner Avenue and Nichols Lane. Included in the column was an observation I made about a pink spray-painted message that was written across a wall inside the church: "I Love Taylor Walsh."

In the midst of the garbage-strewn, weather-beaten, ransacked room, the message stood out as a plaintive, human emotion in the midst of the soggy chaos—and so it was noticed.

Little did I imagine that a couple weeks later, I'd be communicating with Taylor Walsh herself—yes, *that* Taylor Walsh—she who inspired the pink paint avowal.

But it would not have happened had I not received a note from a young man in Huntington Beach. He explained to me his fascination with old, abandoned buildings. He described how, sometimes, he finds access into these places. Not to steal. Not to ransack. But, rather, to imagine what the history may have been like in the building, to take photos and to study the past.

"I've always had a passion for historical buildings," he wrote, "especially in Huntington Beach where I've lived the majority of my life. I enjoy finding out about what buildings have stood the test of time, what buildings use to be used for, and learning about abandoned buildings."

As well, he'd never entered a sealed-off structure with the intent to spray paint. But last year, his love of a local girl got the better of him.

Another excerpt from the letter: "I wanted to say I'm sorry because I spray-painted 'I Love Taylor Walsh,' on the inside of that church—at that time breaking in to historic buildings, Tay, and Writing were the three most important things in my life, and they still are. The reason I am apologizing though is because at the time I had heard that they were going to tear it down, and this upset me. I loved that building and that mural."

The spray-painted sign proclaiming love for Taylor Walsh.

Daniel (last name withheld by request), who wrote the letter, also explained at length about some of the other places he had "visited" over the years. Familiar with some of the books I've written about historic places, Daniel felt I might empathize to a degree with his numerous wanderings to off-limits places.

And to a degree, admittedly, I do. While I will not condone trespassing, truth be told, I have ventured occasionally into places that I know will soon be gone for the purpose of documentation. Sometimes, the siren call of the past is simply too strong to resist.

So, at Daniel's request, I agreed to hear more about his story. His lengthy letter to me was heartfelt and well written, and it seemed like the right thing to do.

At Jon's Coffee Shop one morning, we met. Daniel, a recent graduate of Huntington Beach High School, described to me his fascination with old, abandoned places. He showed me photos he's taken inside these places and spoke of some of the things he's discovered (near-new automobiles, homeless camps, etc.). He was earnest, funny and very well spoken. His passion for history was obvious.

As was his passion for Taylor Walsh.

Ms. Walsh, part of a group of high school friends of Daniel's, was not just the object of his eye. "A friend of mine sort of liked her too," he told me.

"And when I heard he was going to ask her to the prom, it really threw me. But we talked it out, and he said he would pass if it meant a lot to me. But I told him it was fine, and so he took her. But it got to me."

Soon after, after deciding to visit the inside of one of his favorite local buildings, the abandoned church, his heart got the better of him. Daniel described how he wanted, in that moment, to document the burning sensation in his heart and soul. He brought the can in with him deliberately, with the intent of adding the message to the wall.

"I figure if they were going to tear it down anyways, I might as well let them know that someone thought the place was beautiful enough to announce their love (with glow-in-the-dark spray paint)."

The can of pink spray paint, used just that once, remains in his spotless car trunk today—evidence of his adoration.

Ms. Walsh learned of the message after reading about it in this column. In fact, she is the one who wrote Daniel and made him aware that I'd written the story in the first place.

She doesn't live in Huntington Beach anymore. But via e-mail, from Ghana no less, she told me this: "When I first saw the article, I actually wasn't mad or upset. It was just rather comical. There's no need to get all worked up over it really."

She also described her move to Africa in August. "My life has changed so dramatically since the move—spiritually, physically, emotionally, mentally. It's the best thing yet the hardest thing I ever done. I loved Huntington Beach and all the friends and family I grew up with, but I always had a yearning to live in Africa as a missionary to serve the people. Instead of dreaming and fantasizing about it, I just went with it."

So there you have it. Two young people who have answered their own calls. Title it the "Ballad of Taylor Walsh," a tale of confession, passion and curiosity, one made possible by technology and, most importantly, facilitated by, for me, what has become one of the most vital institutions left on the planet—the local paper.

(And Daniel has offered to remove the message should the owners request that—though personally I hope it remains as long as the place stands here.)

Chapter 2

"STARS"

HARLOW'S HOUSE

It's no big deal to pass by famed movie star homes while up in Beverly Hills, Benedict Canyon, Bel Air or Holmby Hills. As any star map will show you, certain neighborhoods are rife with celebrity abodes. Down around our beach cities, though, things get a little sparser. Sure, there are Shirley Temple's and John Wayne's old houses in Newport, but beyond that, not much comes to mind. That's why my interest became so piqued last week while I was out taping some new episodes of *Forgotten O.C.*, a series of vignettes on KOCE-TV that features Maria Hall Brown and me exploring the county in search of history. We were going to tape a segment here in Huntington Beach when Maria showed me some information regarding a home with some unusual history. A document from 1976 was headlined "History of the Mystery House Located at (address withheld)."

Then the following information: "Formerly located on top of a hill on Whitney Terrace [which I believe should be 'Whitley'—part of the area known as Whitley Heights], Hollywood, this was the unusual home of the actress Jean Harlow. It had to be removed to make room for a freeway through that area, and was purchased from the state by L.W. 'Blackie' Dye of H.B. in 1949 and moved to its present location where he resided for about 10 years.

"Due to the unusual height of the stucco building, four feet of the top had to be removed for it to pass under the low utility lines on the route to Huntington Beach."

The house believed to have once belonged to silver screen legend Jean Harlow.

At first, there was some controversy about locating such an unusual-looking residence on a lot in that area, but peace was restored after improvements and a paint and stucco job seemed to temper the objections. "Mr. and Mrs. Dick Dusterhoft and their two children now live in the old Harlow home. Dusterhoft has a responsible position with Knott's Berry Farm, and the entire family is active in the First Christian Church of Huntington Beach."

Jean Harlow, if you don't know, was a movie star and became the sex symbol/blonde bombshell whom all others are measured against. From an old bio: "Born in Kansas City, Mo., as Harlean Carpentier. Harlow brought charm and a sexual knowingness to a series of comedies during the 1930s, becoming the model of feminine sexuality in films for the next decade. The original platinum blond, she played the tough working girl whatever her characters' actual social standing, frequently upsetting the decorum of the well-to-do. Her films include *Platinum Blonde* (1931), *Red Dust* (1932), *Bombshell* (1933), *Dinner at Eight* (1933), *Libeled Lady* (1936), and *Saratoga* (1937). She died of uremic poisoning…She was only 26. The film had to be finished by long angle shots using a double.

"[Clark] Gable said he felt like he was in the arms of a ghost during the final touches of the film. Because of her death, the film was a hit. Record numbers of fans poured into America's movie theaters to see the film."

We made our way over to the house to see if we could tape a segment of *Forgotten O.C.* The owners mentioned in the 1976 document, Dick and Sandy Dusterhoft, still live there and were very gracious in allowing us to see the home. (Their children live in the area, and on this day, the Dusterhofts were tending to two grandchildren.)

The home, though rundown thirty-five years ago when they purchased it, has been restored by the Dusterhofts, and today it is beautiful, featuring the classic look of so many other homes still located in Whitley Heights. (Whitley Heights was named for Hobart Johnstone "H.J." Whitley, who developed Whitley Heights, Los Angeles's first celebrity neighborhood, in the 1920s. It's located in the hills above the Hollywood Walk of Fame, north of Franklin Avenue, from Cahuenga Boulevard to Highland Avenue.)

Mrs. Dusterhoft took out a binder bursting with yellowed newspaper clips about the beguiling Ms. Harlow, and there was even a shot of the star atop this very house. As the legend goes (and this house is crammed with legend), Harlow moved here in the 1930s after her marriage fell apart. Clark Gable may have tried knocking the door down to reach the ailing Harlow shortly before she died. The ornate dining room furniture actually belonged to Harlow.

The Dusterhofts clearly enjoy the legacy of the house, pointing out details like where it was cut in two in preparation for the move to Huntington Beach in the 1940s. Walking through the house, noticing the smooth plaster, Spanish-style entryways, tin-panel ceilings and courtyard out back, you almost expect the lithe blonde sex symbol to appear from around a corner. Instead, one of the grandkids pops out and tosses a beach ball.

Rent *Platinum Blonde* or *Red Dust* one of these days. Then think about the fact that one of the last places that a famous Hollywood blonde called home is right here among us, a "Mystery House" where the myth of Jean Harlow still hangs in the air.

Mary McDonough, aka "Erin Walton"

"I was ten years old, and that was my first audition. Imagine, getting a part on *The Waltons* your first time out."

Imagine. But it happened, and Mary McDonough, sitting in a coffee shop near Bolsa Chica Street and Heil Avenue, still appears to be beaming over the experience. Pretty and bright-eyed, the girl millions knew as Erin

Mary McDonough, star of *The Waltons*.

Walton is telling me about an upcoming reunion with the remaining cast members, sort of a floating luncheon that rotates from house to house. She is comfortable telling stories about what it was like entering people's homes for eleven years, portraying a member of one of TV's most beloved families. (She's preparing her autobiography now, and if our hour and a half together is any indication, it will brim with wonderful anecdotes and lessons learned—a study from inside the unique world of what it's like to be a child star and not just survive but thrive.)

Days before, McDonough was back in Los Angeles, taping another episode of the Julia Louis-Dreyfus sitcom *The New Adventures of Old Christine*, on which she portrays Mrs. Wilhoite. She still works steadily as an actress, recently appearing on *ER*, *Boston Legal*, *Will & Grace* and *The West Wing*, among many others, including the Hallmark Channel film *Christmas at Cadillac Jack's*.

She has also worked as an on-camera host and been in numerous commercials, along with having written and directed. But McDonough lives down here in our neck of the woods where, recently, she's begun a series of acting classes for young people.

"They're acting classes," she says, "so obviously they're geared to help young people hone their performance skills. But beyond that, my classes are also designed to help kids deal with things in life. After all, every day we all face challenges that require a certain performance, a certain confidence and belief in oneself, whether it's at school, interviewing for a job or auditioning for a part."

That kind of motivational encouragement comes easily for McDonough, who also travels the country as a life coach, helping adults confront fears so they can thrive both at work and at home. She's energetic and positive, which no doubt plays a big part in how she motivates kids to become better actors and actresses.

"We cover so many things," she says, "like character development, cold reading techniques, auditions, monologues—all the basic training. But most of all, we have fun. We encourage each other, we laugh, we rehearse. I

Mary with her *Waltons* costars as they gathered for a reunion episode.

try and take everything I learned from the industry over the years, all the processes and experiences, and pass them along to the kids."

Classes are broken down into age groups, so there's a five- to eight-year-old group and then a nine- to fourteen-year-old group (with the possibility of some adult classes starting up soon).

Classes are in Huntington Beach and Westminster, and while I won't quote the prices here, I was very surprised at how modest they were for a month's worth compared to what it costs up in Los Angeles (with meetings once per week).

Mary brings an incredible amount of passion, energy and, most of all, experience to her classes, and I think it's a rare chance for kids to work up close and personal with someone of her magnitude. She talks about her parents and how they coped with her near-instant stardom and how, as farm folks from the Midwest, it was tough for them to adapt to the "business." To that end, she also brings lots of insight to how parents can best encourage their kids' love of performance and balance it with sensible expectations.

From Erin Walton to Mrs. Wilhoite and everything in between, McDonough has grown up before our eyes and has become a dedicated teacher of her craft to help nurture the next generation of thespians. I think we're lucky to have her in our midst—a direct descendant from TV's Walton's Mountain.

DEAN TORRENCE

"What better way to end summer?"

Dean Torrence, one half of the legendary 1960s singing duo Jan & Dean, spoke to me recently about the Endless Summer concert he's performing with his band, the Surf City All Stars, this Saturday, September 25, at the Hyatt Regency Huntington Beach Resort & Spa.

And perhaps best of all, it's free.

"That frees us up a bit to do some things we wouldn't normally do," Torrence said. "So we'll play around a bit and also welcome a special guest I have coming out from back east, so look for a few surprises on Saturday night."

Torrence still tours the country in the wake of the 2004 passing of Jan Berry, but obviously the local shows are steeped in even more memories and nostalgia. Part of that is due to the fact that "Surf City," one of Jan & Dean's biggest hits, is also what has become Huntington Beach's official designation ("Surf City USA"). But beyond that, a hometown show for Torrence (who lives right here) is a chance to perform the soundtrack of a generation in one of the exact places that gave birth to the music in the first place.

"Surf culture is still alive and well here," Torrence said, "as are many of the surfers we and the Beach Boys were writing about. We're all a little older, but this still means a lot to all of us."

Talking with Torrence is always interesting because not only has he found himself at the crossroads of so many huge cultural moments, but he remembers them all and is able to tell a story with a wry, self-deprecating tone that is truly entertaining.

Sure, he shared the bill with the Rolling Stones, Marvin Gaye and James Brown on the famed T.A.M.I. Show held in Santa Monica in 1964. Yes, he and Jan had many smash hits on the radio. But Torrence is also a talented graphic designer and out-of-the-box dreamer who, over the years, has had many unique ideas for games shows, variety shows—it just seems he's always a little bit ahead of the curve.

"We tried selling the idea of this comedian we sort of discovered back in the early 1970s. Shot a pilot and everything. Nobody cared. Until a few years later when that same comedian, Steve Martin, was making millions in movies like *The Jerk*."

Torrence shrugs that off, along with a host other ideas that, to hear him describe, all seem like blockbusters. But timing got in the way.

"I'd say usually, I'm about three to four years ahead of the curve," he chuckled philosophically.

The author, *at right*, pictured with singing legend and Huntington Beach local Dean Torrence.

Fortunately, Torrence is working on a book about his life, and excerpts are available today at his website, www.jananddean.com.

We're lucky to have a rock-and-roll legend living in our midst, and that's why I hope a lot of people take advantage of the opportunity to hear Torrence for free this Saturday. No doubt the crowd will know every lyric to every song and will recall vividly where they were when they first heard them.

"Car radios," Torrence told me. "That's where this generation grew up on music and developed these deeply emotional connections to the songs. That's how it was then, the radios and then the records they'd buy after hearing the songs on the radio. It was a much simpler time. Today, kids have so many options when it comes to music. That's great, but I wonder if, in forty years, they'll be connected to the music of their youth like our fans are."

Torrence works hard to make his concerts authentic beach parties that will make concertgoers feel as if they have been transported to a retro beach party, back to a time of innocence and simple pleasures.

"There's so much magic left in that early '60s music," he said. "People remember the Beach Boys and us and a whole lot of other singers that gave them the soundtrack of their lives at all those critical moments growing up. When you play for people today, you can see them reliving the most important moments of their youth."

EVE PLUMB, AKA JAN BRADY

"People ask me, 'Do you care if people buy one of your paintings because you're Jan Brady?' I say, 'No, their money is still the same!'" And with a girlish laugh, the attractive artist reveals, for a moment at least, a notable part of her past. But, refreshingly, she'll never dwell on it.

Recently in this column, you read about Mary McDonough, who played Erin on *The Waltons* and now lives locally and teaches acting to local youngsters (while still working in Hollywood). As if having one 1970s TV icon nearby wasn't enough, Mary told me about her friend Eve Plumb living nearby in Laguna Beach. But on this day, here is Eve Plumb right here in Huntington Beach, talking about art, *The Brady Bunch* and acting—but mostly art, because that's what she does today and that's what is important to her.

In a day and age when many TV icons spend so much time managing and dealing with their past, Eve has moved gracefully forward, letting the past be just that.

Staring thoughtfully at her mug of coffee, she speaks with the philosophical weariness of someone who has lived it. "It's hard to get away from it sometimes," she says. "If you let your past define you, it can drive you crazy. My attitude is, find the good in it, work it into what you do now and that's enough. I don't have a big interest in constantly living in the past."

Of course, one could easily forgive her if she did choose to wrap herself in the characters she brought to life over the years. Already something of a veteran child actor ("I could read and cry on cue when I was very young,"

she says. "That helped a lot.") by the time she was cast as Jan Brady in 1969, post-Brady, Ms. Plumb also starred in the made-for-TV movie *Dawn—Portrait of a Teenage Runaway*, *Little Women* and many other productions. She still acts today when the part is right but is far more at home with her paints, brushes and canvases than she is with scripts and auditions.

Eve Plumb, artist and actress who many may remember as Jan Brady from *The Brady Bunch*.

Her still life paintings (some of which are viewable online in a special gallery created for this column) are simple, elegant and introspective. "People suggest I do *Brady Bunch* stuff," she chuckles. "But since I don't think about it that much, it doesn't really factor in my paintings. What inspires me more is my love of history, love of vintage things—and small, intimate moments from life." How does she compare acting versus painting? "They both have emotional setbacks," she offers. "With the art, like acting, you set yourself up for rejection, pain—but you have to do it—that's all part of the process."

Eve painted as a child and a teenager, and as she grew, the self-taught artist absorbed as much as she could while visiting museums and studying some of her favorites, including Norman Rockwell, along with a host of contemporary artists. Today, her work is on display at various galleries around the country, and special exhibits of her paintings are becoming more and more frequent.

If you're wondering, Eve is still in touch with Christopher Knight ("Peter Brady") from the show and occasionally crosses paths with her other TV siblings. But for her these days, she is focused on being an artist in Laguna Beach (she's married, no children). However, as much as she looks to the future, and as much as she grows and evolves as a painter, fond moments from the past will no doubt sneak up and tap her on the shoulder. In one moment of nostalgic reflection, Eve smiles to herself and casually tosses out a memory or two.

"I loved working with Lassie," she says. "And Barbara Stanwyck, Lucille Ball—so many others. If I only knew then what I was in the middle of! Those were nice days back then. When I wasn't working, we'd visit Laguna, and it was like our vacation getaway. The farms, the fields—I loved driving down here to Orange County from Los Angeles. It had such western charm and the sense of romance and early soul of California—I loved it. I think Knott's Berry Farm was my favorite—the schoolhouse, the button museum, panning for gold. I remember they had us *Brady* kids, when we had a singing act, perform there at Knott's in the old John Wayne Theater. The train goes around back, and we'd always put pennies on the track. Then Susan Olsen (who played Cindy Brady) and I would put old-fashioned bonnets on so we could go on rides in disguise and nobody would know it was us."

And, of course, she's frequently reminded of the effect she's had on popular culture. "I was lucky to have a nice character, Jan Brady," she says. "But what's weird is how all of these people come up to me and say, 'I grew up with you'—yet they're much younger than me!" She laughs once more, a TV icon who's thankful for her other creative talents.

A HITCHCOCK MYSTERY

When I was about twelve years old, the first time I visited California from New York, I ran smack into Alfred Hitchcock's stomach.

Our family vacation was officially underway as my parents checked us into the Century Plaza hotel in Los Angeles. My two sisters and I were knocking around the lobby, burning off some post-flight steam, and I didn't see him coming through the front door.

After bouncing off his gut, I recognized him almost instantly—not because I was a young film buff but, rather, because I'd just seen him interviewed on TV a few days earlier. His stern, puffy face was still fresh in my mind, as was his languid British accent. "Young man," he intoned with a deep seriousness, "where are your parents?" With that, he walked me over to my folks, and with an admonition along the lines of, "Young men should behave properly in public," he actually patted my head and moved on. Talk about a welcome to the West Coast.

That event may be why I became such an avid student of the wonderful artist. But whatever the reason, many of his movies seem to grow in stature and impact the more I see them. I bring this up because the Oscars are on this weekend, and each Oscar season, when so much focus is on movies, I remind myself of just how great Alfred Hitchcock was. What makes this year special is that I recently learned of a connection that Huntington Beach shares with the master of suspense.

To begin, though, did you know that, outside of an honorary statuette in 1968, Hitchcock never won the award? It's true, the famed director of *Rear Window* (1954), *Vertigo* (1958), *North by Northwest* (1959) and *Psycho* (1960) was completely shut out after being nominated five times. The only movie directed by Hitchcock to win the Academy Award for Best Picture was *Rebecca* (1940), the very first film he directed in the United States.

But awards or no, to me no one can touch Hitchcock. His best films retain a look and feel that has proven to be timeless. But besides Hitchcock, who was responsible for the taut, classic texture that seems burned into every inch of celluloid? Director of Photography Robert Burks, ASC. Hitchcock first worked with Burks in 1950, making the classic *Strangers on a Train*, and the chemistry was instant.

The film earned Burks Hitchcock's respect, as well as an Academy Award nomination. Burks proved to be the perfect cinematographer for Hitchcock. For the next fourteen years, Burks photographed eleven more of Hitchcock's best-known suspense classics, including *I Confess* (1953), *Dial*

M for Murder (1954), *Rear Window* (1954), *To Catch a Thief* (1955), *The Trouble with Harry* (1955), *The Man Who Knew Too Much* (1956), *The Wrong Man* (1957), *Vertigo* (1958), *North by Northwest* (1959), *The Birds* (1963) and *Marnie* (1964).

I asked Aaron Leventhal, co-author of the excellent book *Footsteps in the Fog* from Santa Monica Press, about the importance of the collaboration. "Robert Burks's cinematography helped bring to life some of the most well-known and revered Alfred Hitchcock films," he said. "Burks and Hitchcock worked together over two decades, marking a collaboration that witnessed some of the great master works of Hitchcock's career, and possibility even a partnership and vision that remains unequaled today."

Legendary filmmaker Alfred Hitchcock, whose cinematographer is laid to rest right here in Huntington Beach.

Burks's work on *To Catch a Thief* earned him an Academy Award, putting him one up on the great director. In twenty-five years as a director of photography, Burks made fifty-five features.

Sadly, his collaborations with Hitchcock ended on May 13, 1968. That's when Burks and his wife, Elizabeth, died in a fire at their home in Newport Beach. So what's the Huntington Beach connection? Well, if you ever visit the Good Shepherd Cemetery on Talbert Avenue, at Section D, Lot 1409, Grave 5, you'll see he's laid to rest here. I've been trying to find out if he has relatives here, maybe his children, but so far I haven't been able to make the connection.

But no matter, he's a film legend. I didn't see many of the things nominated this year, nor do I care to. I'll probably watch the show (or at least part of it), but first I'll go lay a bouquet in honor of Hitchcock's right-hand man—it's the least I can do for all that great work. Then I'll go home and maybe watch *North by Northwest*.

LIVING DOLL

Franki Doll, rock star and mom.

"The store was packed. We played a good show. The next thing you know, I'm getting a message saying, 'You're going to be in Hot Topic. You're the perfect fit, we're excited and we hope you are too.'"

Singer/songwriter Franki Doll is recounting what may turn out to be a life-changing moment: a recent performance that sealed a particularly sweet deal for her band, Huntington Beach–based Franki Doll and the Broken Toys.

Hot Topic, the popular mall-based rock-and-roll clothing and accessories retail chain, has a unique history of showcasing in-store band competitions, in search of breakthrough acts. Once they pick a winner, the chosen band's CDs are featured in store, the band tours throughout the company's 688 national locations—and exposure can go through the roof. That's why the call to Franki meant so much. "We played there, as a lot of bands do, and I guess we stood out. We brought people in. Owl City, Paramore—some good bands have come out of this, and so we were blown away. We have sixty thousand fans on MySpace, so this is a good time and a good way for our first official CD to get introduced."

Franki and the band are working on that now, and in the meantime, the strikingly pretty, lithe lead singer is taking a deep, figurative pause in life so the meaning of the moment is not lost on her. Sitting over coffee last week (early morning after a triumphant gig the night before at the Coach House in San Juan Capistrano), she is a riddle inside a paradox wrapped up in a mystery.

After all, Franki Doll is not your average rock-and-roll front person. Sure, she may look the part, with her pink-streaked, jet black hair and tattoos—one part Patti Smith, one part Joan Jett and one part Pat Benatar. She may act the part too, because after all, she and the Broken Toys were voted best live band at a recent Orange County Music Awards show (and Franki was named "Most Memorable Front Person"), best live punk band—among other accolades. But Franki goes far beyond any sort of rock-and-roll stereotyping. You see, Franki, in addition to fronting the Broken Toys, also has three teenage children (ages fifteen, seventeen and nineteen). And for all of her rock-and-roll flash, power and beauty, when she describes her kids, this woman's heart and soul come through like nothing else. "I am just so proud of them," she says. "They're amazing kids, and I think they're excited with what's happening now with my music."

Looking at her, it doesn't seem possible. You might guess Franki is in her twenties. But then again, Franki doesn't get hung up on how things should "look." "I know I don't look like a PTA mom when I go to school functions. But if people just closed their eyes before judging me, I think they'd find I'm just another mom who cares for her kids. This is just who I am. I've never smoked, drank or done drugs. People read so much into appearances. But this is just who I am."

Franki's upbringing presented many challenges. A broken household, winding up in a foster home and many other cold, cruel moments for a little girl who loved to sing seem to have made her stronger and given her purpose. Today, she goes and speaks to kids on the edge. She has a plan to create incentives for her fan base to do good, meaningful things in the world. And most of all, she looks to move people through her music.

Her current band, the Broken Toys (Jenson Avery, drums; Chris Khaos, guitar; Alex Smith, guitar; and Andy Montana, bass), has been together five years. Coming out of the Huntington Beach scene that was crystallized by the band Avenged Sevenfold (several of whom are friends of Franki's), the group seems poised and ready for the next level.

Franki (whose eclectic musical tastes run the gamut from the Sex Pistols to Styx to James Taylor) is ready for sure. And for the right reasons.

"Life presented me with all sorts of challenges," she says in her schoolgirl voice. But despite her youthful tone, the words flow with a wise, insightful knowing. "My mom got back in touch with me recently. That was hard, a little scary, but important to me. I try to make sense of everything in my life right now, and it will definitely come through the music, like it always does,"

She talks about a recent performance in Hot Topic: "We were playing our song 'Suffocated Light.' It's about people trying to dim other people but then standing up to those people and being responsible for who you are. We stopped playing the music and just let the people sing the words: 'Stand on your own and own what you've become.' It was awesome. They sang the lyric over and over, making it their own song. It got so emotional some people were crying."

No challenges yet in life have been able to quell the passion and fire that Franki Doll feels in her music. And that's a good thing. When you or your kids start to see the new CD in Hot Topic, I hope you check it out. I have no doubt it will rock. But I'm also sure it will have soul, purpose and meaning. Because that's what Franki Doll is all about.

STEVE HAYES

"I was working at Googies the Sunday Dean was killed, and as you now know, I knew him fairly well, and I swear it was as if a meteor had crashed into Hollywood killing thousands. People on the street who had no connection to the industry were weeping."

He's referring to James Dean.

"Same with Monroe. I knew women who wore black for weeks in mourning. My then-wife, Janet, summed it up perfectly when she said, 'Hell, had she known it would cause this much of a stir, she would have killed herself years ago!' And remember, Janet and I knew her pretty well."

That's Marilyn Monroe.

Meet Steve Hayes, author, actor, painter and raconteur so exceptionally blessed with the art of storytelling (and life experiences) that he's already filled two books of memoirs, *Googies, Coffeeshop to the Stars* parts one and two.

If you didn't know, Googies was a famous Hollywood haunt back in the glamorous 1940s and '50s, a hot spot where Hayes worked for a number of years. When he wasn't acting. Or living with Errol Flynn. Or squiring Ava Gardner around town when Sinatra was out of town. When he wasn't with Tyrone Power, Lana Turner or the aforementioned Dean and Monroe. Or when he wasn't in Cuba with Castro and Hemingway.

Hayes's life is almost comically rich with provocative, romantic escapades and adventures. But as interesting as his past is, it's his current and no doubt his future that, to me, make him most compelling.

I met Steve last week at the Starbucks on Goldenwest near Yorktown. It was 7:00 a.m., and he'd just finished up at the gym. He works out there from about 4:00 to 6:00 a.m., six days a week.

And he's eighty-one years old.

I almost omitted that fact, because it really adds little to this story. See, when you meet Steve, you'd probably guess he's about sixty or so. Then again, the firm grip, boundless conversational energy and electric twinkle in his eyes might have you shave off yet another half decade. This isn't a story about age. It's about attitude.

He told me he's conditioned to need only several hours of sleep each night after being awakened so often as a little boy growing up in war-torn England. "The bombing raids were murder for sleep," he chuckled in a polished, somewhat devilish laugh.

Back in the 1950s, Hayes's dashing, matinee-idol looks landed him plenty of small parts. But the writer in him won out, and to date, he's penned countless screenplays for TV and film, almost two dozen fiction books and his two-part, all-but-impossible-to-put-down memoir.

Hayes moved to Huntington Beach in the last decade with his wife of twenty-five years, Robbin. While he obviously finds life quieter and more laid-back than those tumultuous eras in Tinseltown, he also knows that the curtain came down on that world a long time ago.

"Once the studio system went away, the business changed," he said. "It used to be, every day, you'd see the biggest stars every day at the studios. Then at the nightclubs in the evening. It was another world back then."

Because he was younger than many of his counterparts when he first came over from England, he's also outlived most of them—and so he remains a vital connection to the days of Ciro's, the Trocadero and all the other mythical places from Hollywood's most golden era. Couple that with his exceptional ability to recount rich details and dialogue, and you have simply one of the most interesting people anyone would ever want to meet.

Rather than dwell too much on the past though, Hayes lays out his next month. More writing, some speaking engagements, a showing of some of his paintings—and, of course, lots of exercise.

I wondered if he gets asked what his secret for youth is, beyond his clearly insatiable, act-how-you-feel zest for life and getting things done. "Don't inhibit yourself," he said. "Do what you're supposed to be doing—not what they tell you they think you are supposed to be doing." By "they," he no doubt is referring to anyone who dares try to put you in a box and make you behave by some predetermined societal standard.

I keep pausing in writing this column to read more of Steve's memoirs. The Sunset Strip comes to life on so many levels through his razor-sharp memories: the excitement, the pain, the struggle, the redemption—all the elements of the pleasure dome recounted in such powerful first-person voice that you may feel like you've been transported there yourself. Back when a galaxy of stars ruled the world.

Steve's books are available on Amazon.com. I cannot recommend them enough.

But what I would most recommend, if ever possible (and if he ever slows down), is that you sit down for a cup of coffee with Steve Hayes.

A most remarkable young man.

OLGA

Her eyes twinkle in the morning sun, and her smile beams. Looking out across the water while standing on the boardwalk at the Bolsa Chica wetlands, she glances up as a large pelican swoops by, just several feet over our heads. She laughs like a girl decades younger than seventy-eight, but then, age doesn't really mean too much to Olga Connolly.

Born Olga Fikotová, in 1956 she won a gold medal in the discus competition at the 1956 Olympic games held in Melbourne, Australia. Also at these games, Olga met and fell in love with well-known American athlete Harold Connolly.

No less than the *New York Times* editorialized: "The H-bomb overhangs us like a cloud of doom. The subway during rush hours is almost impossible to endure. But Olga and Harold are in love, and the world does not say no to them."

Back home in her native Czechoslovakia, the couple's romance, not the gold medal, got the headlines. Accused of being a traitor by the Communist authorities, Olga's marriage to Harold represented the end of her career as a Czechoslovak athlete. But that didn't stop her. Olga became a U.S. citizen and went on to represent her new country at four Olympic games. So respected was she by her teammates that Olga was chosen to carry the U.S. flag at the opening ceremony of the 1972 Munich Olympics in Munich, Germany.

Throughout her career, Olga captured five U.S. national titles and raised the American record no fewer than four times, adding over fifteen feet to the previous record.

Olga and Harold Connolly were divorced in the mid-'70s, but their children certainly carried on the athletic legacy of the family. One of their sons became a nationally known javelin thrower and decathlete, while one of their daughters played on the U.S. national volleyball team. (Harold Connolly passed away last year at the age of seventy-nine.)

Olga has lived in Huntington Beach for two years. Several months ago, she joined the Miracles of the Marsh docent team from the Bolsa Chica Land Trust. She meets at the wetlands most weeks to teach visiting school kids about nature. As

Olga Connolly as she looks today.

she wistfully described, nature, as much as athletics, has always played a big part in her life.

"Since I was a young girl in Czechoslovakia, I've always respected nature. The peace and solitude, the sound of the streams on the rocks; it's always been vital to my life. I explain to my grandkids today what it was like to wander, plucking seeds from the ripening wheat and munching on them in the beautiful fields. It's so hard to find open places today. That's why I love it here."

Entranced by the wetlands after moving here, the environmentally conscious Connolly realized she had a connection to the place where she'd often walk, jog and simply get lost in the beautiful sights and sounds.

"In the early 1990s, I received a request to write a letter on behalf of protecting these wetlands. I was living in Culver City then and did not know anything about them. After I first visited here a couple of years ago, I realized, this was the exact place I'd written about."

Then, while wandering here one day, she met a man who was selling calendars on behalf of the Land Trust. They got to talking, and then Connolly, a former California Conservation board member and accomplished environmental activist, decided to get involved by becoming a docent to help educate the visiting students.

"I thought I knew a lot until they started training me," she laughed. "But they are so knowledgeable and dedicated; I realized I had a lot to learn."

But she learned everything she needed to know to lead the kids, which she does today with great joy. Then again, she seems to do everything with great joy.

"I teach fitness classes at UCI, I teach many private students, and I tell everyone the same thing: you must enjoy exercise. Without joy, you won't approach it with passion. I see people today jogging and working and they look like they are at war—all serious and intense. No smile, no joy. It looks like work. For me, whether it was the discus, or jogging, or anything health related, joy played a big part."

She still speaks with a pronounced Czech accent in a warm voice that exudes charm, wisdom and curiosity. And she has a mission beyond just the wetlands: "Kids today are not in shape like they used to be. They worship high-paid professional athletes, but they don't get out and play the sports on their own. We have to make sure, as parents and teachers, that we help children learn the importance of health and exercise and how to enjoy it."

That she shows no sign of slowing down at seventy-eight simply illustrates her life philosophy.

"Age is simply what you make of it," she said. The fit, energetic, eternally girlish Olympian gazed about the wetlands. "We need room for the human spirit to roam," she stated quietly. "It's in our nature. It's why places like this must be protected. And why we must teach children not just the importance of exercise and fitness but of appreciating nature."

Chapter 3

ANIMALS

DEAR VERONICA

Nine Christmases ago, we found a package from Santa near the tree: a cat. Not a kitten but a full-grown, full-bodied snowshoe. The kids were delighted; they'd never had a dog or cat. My wife was thrilled. Me, I'm not a cat person, so I was happy for everyone else. As I soon learned though, this was no ordinary cat.

Veronica, as we named her, was not selfishly aloof, as many cats get stereotyped. She was an elegant, affectionate animal who in no time flat decided that my office would be where she'd spend her days. As I wrote at my computer, she'd ascend into my lap to sleep or sometimes pat on the keys with her paws. She reminded me of the "all work and no play" adage, coaxing me to the floor to tease her with her stuffed fish or a piece of yarn. Veronica became the best pet I have ever known, and I've had some good ones. Four years ago, when our adopted puppy entered the picture, Veronica wasn't too happy, but over time, they formed a fragile bond.

As she got older, Veronica came downstairs less, claiming an upstairs alcove as her space and, eventually, our bed, which was fine. In the last year or so, she played less—she was almost seventeen, after all—but was still this noble, seemingly wise creature whose purrs were so deep and steady that you couldn't help but wonder what she was thinking about.

This holiday season, Veronica's health started to seriously falter. She was losing weight and slowing down. Her purrs became a wheeze, and she became very weak. We took her to the Animal Hospital of Huntington Beach. The doctor took X-rays and then told us that cancer was consuming her, suffocating her, and that her life, most likely, could not even be measured in days. We all sat there, numb. I think we all knew in the bottom of our hearts (and the pits of our stomachs) what the most humane decision was. Still, this was Veronica—how could this be the end?

We'd never had to put an animal down before, but as a family, we accepted the hard reality.

I don't equate animals with humans, and I have lost people very close to me. But I'd also forgotten what it is like when a family pet becomes family, as Veronica certainly had. Weeping over her, we remembered the day we got her and the instant joy she brought to our house. As the kids held her, those beautiful purrs came back once more, fleetingly, as if to force a last goodbye. We wept. We apologized. We prayed over her. We said goodbye.

The kids, trembling, spent a last quiet moment with her and then left the room. My wife and I stayed for the procedure, but as they prepared to fix the needle into the catheter affixed to her paw, in those last seconds, the memories flooded forth: seeing her with the kids as they grew; welcoming us home from vacations with long, emotional meows; warming by the fire as she got older; sleeping on my orange sweatshirt in the cardboard box in my office; patiently letting my wife bathe her in the kitchen sink; coming home from her "spa treatment" with a big pink bow on her collar—and this final day, where, all of a sudden, she seemed to be calling for help. In just a few seconds, she was lifeless on the table. She was gone. Just like that. Our beautiful Veronica.

She will always be part of our family—a most special Christmas package that blessed our household for nine splendid years.

Goodbye, Veronica. We'll always miss you. We'll always love you.

I should mention how compassionate and professional the staff at the Animal Hospital of Huntington Beach were—exceptional people, one and all.

While there, our kids had some extra unexpected help coping with our loss. In the waiting area, they became distracted by a mini-warrior named Nigel, an abandoned kitten just a couple months old who'd been dumped at a local shelter with a mohawk shaved so deep into his fur that they told us you could see the razor marks.

As we all hugged, Nigel's feisty little swipes from his cage provided just the distraction the kids needed in that moment. Then they held him, he

The Epting family cat, Veronica.

purred and that little critter seemed to do the impossible: he made them feel a little better.

My wife and I thought that maybe fate was having its way, placing him in our path. I know it's not wise to replace pets as a knee-jerk response, but this would be no replacement—this was an abandoned, abused baby animal that needed a home. Without telling the kids, Jean and I conspired.

As I type this, I can hear his little bell as he bounces around our bedroom, exploring his new home. Whether we discovered a needy animal or an animal discovered a needy us, I don't know. But I'm thankful he's here, and I'm especially thankful for that Christmas morning nine years ago when our lives changed for the better all because of a cat named Veronica.

As you all reflect, rejoice and celebrate your loved ones both here and gone—to all of you (family pets included), merry Christmas from the Eptings: myself, Jean, Charlie, Claire and my mom, Louise.

And in what's become a bit of a tradition, this is the Christmas poem our daughter, Claire, wrote three years ago for this column.

What happened this night was so much to behold,
Out here in the shivering cold.
To see what I saw,
To have known what I know,
To hear what I heard,
Is greater than gold.
Star light, star bright, an angel appeared,
In God's glory there was so much to be feared.
But the angel said, "Do not be afraid,
For Mary, the lowly handmaid,
Is to bear a son who shall save us all.
So go there to see the Lord,
Follow the star that is ever so tall."
So we headed forth to see what is to see,
All amazed at what the angel had told us what He is to be.
There at the manger, to my surprise,
The baby was there, I couldn't believe my eyes!
And then I felt a feeling so strong!
And I knew that He was Jesus Christ,
the Messiah, whom we had been waiting for ever so long!
So what happened that night, that glorious sight,
Is what I will always believe,
And that is just what happened on Christmas Eve.

Dog Beach

After hearing the about the loss of my friend Martin Senat (one of the founders of Dog Beach) last week, I found this piece I'd written for a local blog years ago:

I used to roll my eyes a bit when we'd drive past Dog Beach. "Do dogs need that much beach?" "Isn't it a bit excessive?" "Is it clean?"

Then we adopted a dog. One visit, and I was hooked. Sure, it's good for the dogs, who get a blissful sensory overload of sand, salty water and other dogs. But I think Dog Beach might be even better for the people who bring the dogs. This tucked-away stretch of sand seems to function as its own little Utopia. People seem relaxed, civil and even thoughtful as they watch their hounds bound in the surf.

Soon after, here "In the Pipeline," I wrote a piece that documented a trip I'd made to Jamestown, North Dakota. While there, I'd met someone who'd just returned from Southern California. What did they rave about most from their visit? Dog Beach.

Then I learned that the future of Dog Beach as we knew it was in jeopardy.

That's how I got to know Martin. He'd called me one day, gravely concerned that the city was trying to put Dog Beach out of business. While his concerns may have been overstated, clearly the city had started making a

A flyer available at Dog Beach.

few demands of Martin that would have seriously impeded his ability to run things the way he was used to. After the column ran, based on even a remote possibility of Dog Beach being harmed, it helped ignite a debate between Senat and the city that he eventually seemed to win. He pled his case eloquently and humanely throughout the process. His compassionate tenacity, fueled by his love of animals, was a stunning thing to behold.

Martin was also aware that not everyone was behind the concept of a dog beach. More than once I'd received a call or e-mail from him alerting me to the fact that someone was complaining. Perhaps a city council person or a disgruntled local who simply did not understand the charms of a beach for dogs.

Whatever it was, whenever he felt that his haven might be under attack, he'd reach out. First to catch up on life and then to try and enlist some help in defense of his organization.

Martin was easy to go to bat for—a good man whose heart was in the right place. If you ever saw him at Dog Beach, you'd know what I mean. To watch Martin walk Dog Beach was to watch a great conductor direct his favorite orchestra. He engaged nearly everyone who walked by; checked the bag dispensers and then dispensed with treats for passing pups; gave away T-shirts; offered quips, bits of gossip and wry observations—he was as at home at Dog Beach as the dogs themselves.

And the place will just never be the same without my charming, erudite British friend.

His daughter Simone left this message on her dad's Facebook page: "So blessed to have walked this journey with you. Your love will forever be in my heart. Thank you for your wisdom and guidance. I love you pops."

The next time you take your dog to the beach, perhaps pause for a moment to remember the man whose effusive spirit and love of animals helped make it possible in the first place. I know I'll always picture him there on the bluff, fussing over his dream, protecting the salty sanctuary he helped organize and tending to his four-legged flock.

We, and the dogs, have lost a lovely man.

Going to the Dogs

It's been a rough couple weeks for professional sports and an even rougher time for quarterback Michael Vick's dogs. I know, I know—he's presumed innocent until proven guilty. That said, eighteen-page federal indictments don't come easy, so for many of us (and devoid of any Vick denials), it's not too big a leap to accept that the brutal acts did probably happen with his approval/involvement.

In the face of the savage behavior outlined in the indictment, I was drawn to a place in Huntington Beach that stands as a testament to people who love their dogs (and other pets)—a place that also helps soothe the feelings of loss that accompany the death of a pet. It's the Sea Breeze Pet Cemetery, and while I doubt you'd ever see Michael Vick or any of his cronies here, you will find sensitive people dedicated to a common cause.

Sea Breeze, which is at Beach Boulevard and Yorktown Avenue, was opened on three spacious acres in 1961 and today is the only pet cemetery in Orange County. Today, it's run by Alan and Brenda Weaver (the original owners were on Alan's side of the family), and Brenda explained one recent morning some of the history and logistics of the peaceful little place created to help celebrate the memories of family pets.

For instance, she detailed how, if you trace the history of the in-ground markers from oldest to most recent, the pet names change with the time—so Spot, Fluffy and Snowball gradually give way to Britney, Amanda and Tyler. Brenda showed me where some of John Wayne's family pets are laid to rest,

The exterior sign at Sea Breeze Pet Cemetery on Beach Boulevard.

along with the dogs of Richard and Karen Carpenter (yes, the Carpenters) and, of course, Sarge, the tough K9 Marine Corps World War II battle dog. Sarge (Major Von Luckner III) even has a shrine inside that includes his flag, Purple Heart and Silver Star medals and a telegram from then-governor Edmund "Pat" Brown offering his sorrow and praise in light of the dog's passing. The sturdy twenty-year-old pooch saved nine wounded men by dragging them to safety during battles and even wore a silver plate in his head, a souvenir of a wartime injury in the South Pacific. Sarge is laid to rest directly in front the main building, and a decorated statue of him sits at attention off to the left.

Strolling the peaceful, well kept, much-decorated grounds, Brenda shows me the exotic pet area, which includes tributes to raccoons, a skunk, a turtle, rabbits—even an eighty-nine-year-old bird (Katie Teeter, 1883–1972) and a chicken (inscription: "Annabel—the hen I grew up with"). But make no mistake, Sea Breeze is mostly about dogs and cats, and the simple inscriptions tell stories of family pets that were truly part of the family. "To our baby girl Gigi—be at peace with God." "Our little angel, Krystal—we miss you and love you." "God has called Snoopy to come home."

Brenda also adds that summer is the busiest time for Sea Breeze, as heat stroke affects so many animals.

If you're wondering, cremations start at about $65, and a full-on plot, marker, etc., everything out-the-door-and-in-the-ground is about $1,000. There's also a small chapel if a family feels like conducting a service with relatives, clergy and friends. Judging from a review of the many markers here, it seems that most families secure a plot for all their pets, not just the most prominent. Dogs are laid to rest beside hamsters, rats and, of course, cats. While there is ample space today, Brenda suggests that at some point the property will be full.

Pet cemeteries have an interesting history in this country. The oldest known one was discovered in Green County, Illinois, by archaeologist Stewart Schrever, who believed pets were interred there around 6500 BC. The oldest operating pet cemetery in the United States is the Hartsdale Pet Cemetery in New York, established in 1896, and the largest pet cemetery in the United States is Bide-A-Wee Home Assn., also in New York.

Whether you have a pet or not, a visit to Sea Breeze is an interesting, calming stop that makes you appreciate the part that pets play within a household. It's also a poignant counterbalance to the brutal news of late. So stop by and take a short walk around. And by all means, pay your respects to Sarge. He's a hero, after all.

For the Pelicans

It is a postcard morning in Huntington Beach: bright yellow sunshine, salt-scented breezes, a few wispy clouds and deep blue waves studded with surfers. Here, where Pacific Coast Highway meets Newland Street, a brown pelican cruises by overhead, pumping silently along a warm breeze toward the wetlands. I wonder if the bird senses the trouble directly below—where fellow pelicans are fighting for their lives.

I had wanted to visit the Wetlands and Wildlife Care Center to document some of the excellent work done there caring for injured and orphaned wildlife throughout Orange County. Tucked in the shadow of the twin power-plant smokestacks, it's easy to miss the small structure as one drives the coast.

What I hadn't counted on was the recent severe outbreak of the toxin called domoic acid, a naturally occurring poison that is produced by microscopic algae in the ocean (the acid accumulates in fish and shellfish and is passed on to other animals as the fish are eaten). I watch as workers treat sick pelicans, feeding them, cleaning them, testing them and keeping them comfortable under soft blankets and warm lamps. With dozens of lifeless birds (including seagulls, loons and cormorants) washing up on shore every day now, it seems these are the lucky ones because they have made it to this soothing sanctuary alive.

Lisa Birkle, the assistant wildlife director at the center, can't recall a domoic acid outbreak this lethal, and she and her volunteer staff have been pushed to the limit. As to why it's so bad this year, some scientists theorize that factors such as overfishing and pollution have allowed the suspect algae to thrive.

Regardless, it is reaching crisis levels. This is on top of what center regulars call "orphan season," the time of year right now when many animal moms are hit by cars, babies fall from trees and other unfortunate circumstances happen that result in hundreds of orphaned baby animals. This is worst case on top of worst case. There's also the regular flow of opossums, raccoons and ground squirrels to tend to.

Wandering through the small, clean facility, one feels like a doctor doing hospital bed checks.

Tired, recuperating pelicans rest patiently and nod a bit as if to acknowledge you.

Outside, dozens of orphaned baby ducks swim together in pristine water and gather to nuzzle an old feather duster—their surrogate mommy. As they

Just a few of the many creatures that have been nursed at the wetlands wildlife center.

grow, they'll graduate to bigger pools, they'll be conditioned to eat properly as they would in the wild and then they'll be released—strong, healthy and eager to get back to their lakes and nests (though they will leave some broken hearts back at the center).

A huge mute swan shares an open space with both a pelican that's nursing a broken wing and some adult ducks; in a nearby cage, a group of feisty ground squirrels climb, crunch nuts and seem to be playing a form of "squirrel tag." Several rows down, seven silent, curious raccoons spill out of their domed house to greet this visitor. The sunshine and ocean air seem to add to the therapeutic nature of the center, and all the animals out here appear to be thriving.

For more than seventeen years, the center has cared for around twenty thousand critters, thanks in large part to a seasoned volunteer staff, people like Lisa and Greg Hickman. Hickman, the center manager, has a storied career of caring for wildlife. It goes back to the old Lion Country Safari in Irvine, then to Anaheim and eventually this renowned educator wound his way here to Huntington Beach in 1990. That was the year 400,000 gallons of Alaskan Crude spilled off the Surf City coast. A makeshift facility was set up here to tend to the many sick birds, and then in 1998, the Wetlands and Wildlife Care Center was officially christened.

The burly, affable Hickman doesn't want to talk about the past though. For him it's the future that matters, and with good reason. This summer, adjacent to the center, their new animal hospital and interpretive center opens. In what will certainly become a much-visited place, the state-of-the-art facility will blend science, medicine, technology and public learning in a manner that's unprecedented for the area. Hickman smiles as we tour the soon-to-open building, and he's clear about what this center means, beyond functioning as a world-class hospital.

"We'll take care of lots of wildlife here with some of the world's best experts," Hickman said. "But this is where generations of kids will learn why these things are so important. Hopefully, this will shape their view of nature now so that when they grow up they'll be able to do the right things. We'll have displays, incredible information, teaching areas—we'll want people to come here as much as they'd like. And we can't wait for the field trips."

It's clear that this center is destined to become one of our city's most important centers.

Back at the old building, volunteers work calmly and carefully, feeding and washing sick pelicans, while Lisa feeds an injured hummingbird. Out back, ducklings huddle around their momma feather duster and splash in the water. A volunteer on the phone advises a caller not to feed ducks in her pool or to pick up ducklings because mom might abandon them. (The questions regarding how to deal with backyard wildlife are too numerous to cover here, but the center will be happy to help you.)

It's business as usual at a place you might not have noticed before—a small shelter by the side of the road that's full of big hearts; a place where orphans are mothered, the injured are mended and the sick are healed.

GRUNION RUN

For years since we moved to Huntington Beach, I have wanted to go on a grunion run. So when the call came last week that Bill Burhans, a seasonal interpretive specialist for the Department of Parks and Recreation, would be leading a small group of Amigo de Bolsa Chica members along the beach one night at 11:30 p.m., I happily tagged along (with my son in tow).

Now, you may have read Vic Leipzig and Lou Murray's column last week about how successful the trip was. They were there; they know what we all witnessed. But it was so spectacular, I thought I'd add to the mix with this column. I've heard from so many people over the years who have spent many a late night in search of the elusive grunion, only to come home tired, wet and grunionless, so I wanted to reiterate the hope that grunions spring eternal in Huntington Beach.

Some background from the definitive grunion site, www.grunion.org: "California grunion are a species of marine fish found only along the coast of Southern California and northern Baja California. They are justifiably famous for their unique spawning behavior. Grunion spawn completely out of the water and lay their eggs on many sandy beaches in California. Shortly after high tide, on specific nights, sections of these beaches sometimes are covered with thousands of grunion dancing about on the sand. The popularity of these grunion runs means that some nights there are more people lining the beaches than grunion in the run."

Now, there's no guarantee that any grunion will appear on said nights, but if they do, this is what happens afterward: "The eggs remain buried in the sand throughout incubation, fully out of water for approximately two weeks. The larvae hatch when the eggs wash out by high waves during tides before the new and full moons. Grunion spawn at the age of one year, and live for two to four years. Because of their vulnerability during the spawning season, they are protected by a closed season. No taking of grunion is permitted during April and May. During other months, no gear is permitted so collection may take place only with bare hands, and a fishing license is required."

One of the many grunions we encountered this particular evening.

So, those are your grunion basics. And if you want to have perhaps the ultimate grunion experience, I'd recommend a trip with Burhans. After all, he's four for four this season—that's right, all four nights he's gone out to the beach on a run he's seen grunions. But nothing like last week. "The best count I have seen was with you and the Amigos de Bolsa Chica on May 26," he told me.

And it might have to do with the spot where we were looking. He'd never been there before on a grunion run, but his hunches paid off, and as tens of thousands of bouncing silvery beauties came in with the midnight tide, he got excited. All of a sudden, a motto change from "Surf City" to "Grunion City" seemed like it might be in order.

Where exactly were we? I'm going to withhold that information for now, at the risk of inciting grunion chaos. But if you get ahold of Burhans, I'm sure he'll lead you there.

Burhans has been volunteering at Bolsa Chica since the summer he retired from teaching in 2003. Most of his thirty-year teaching career had been as a middle school science teacher with Long Beach Unified, and he uses his teaching skills well when schooling prospective grunion viewers along the shore.

"Bolsa Chica State Beach became a participant of the Grunion Greeter Project in 2005," he said. "Dr. Karen Martin of Pepperdine University is the project director. Each season, we have approximately ten nights of monitoring on schedule. These are usually two nights after the full moon or new moon high tide. The best time for grunion observation begins in mid-April and lasts until the end of June."

So there's still time, Huntington Beach, and if you see half the grunion count we saw May 26, you will still be awed. Some other tips, should you decide to go:

- Dress warmly.
- Wear shoes you don't mind getting wet.
- Bring a flashlight, but try not to use it until you know that the grunion have arrived. They will shy away from light and noise.
- This program is more of a scientific observation than the actual catching of the grunion.
- If you plan to catch grunion, licenses are required for those sixteen and older.

Finally, according to Bill, "In looking for other locations to observe grunion, I would look for isolated, gently sloping beach."

Driving past the beach the day after the run was surreal. If only those joggers and bike riders knew what had been there just several hours before, swimming, slithering and spawning, while most of the city slept.

SERRANO THE HORSE

For decades, he mystified and thrilled audiences, displaying psychic feats of unparalleled ability. Billed variously as the "World's Best Educated Horse" and the "Psychic Horse with the College Education," the equine known as Serrano was a worldwide legend through the 1940 and '50s, guessing ages, unscrambling words, finding objects under boxes and picking objects by color.

Born along the banks of the Santa Ana River in the 1940s, Serrano was quite the celebrity back then. He appeared on the TV show *You Asked for It* and continuously toured county and state fairs all over the country, making as much as $1,000 a day from people who thought they could stump him. A popular contest was to ask an audience member to step forward and concentrate hard on his own age. Then, using numbered blocks, the great Serrano would choose the two that matched the participant's age.

Owned by local farmer and horseman Clint Brush, Serrano wound up becoming a popular feature act at Knott's Berry Farm, performing there throughout the 1950s and '60s (back when Knott's featured other charming attractions such as the organ grinder, the seal pool, the bee exhibit, glow-in-the-dark rocks and the glow-in-the-dark Jesus from the Chapel of Reflections).

Serrano, the world's best-educated horse, as he looked when he lived in Huntington Beach.

But some of you might remember that Serrano lived right here in Huntington Beach, at the Brush barn located at Beach Boulevard and Heil Avenue.

Craig Hoxie, a Huntington Beach crime scene investigator who grew up in the area, remembers meeting Serrano at Knott's. "When I was about seven, in the late 1960s, they picked me out of the crowd for Serrano to guess my age. And he did it! He counted off my age correctly by scratching his hoof into the dirt. I didn't see my dad signal my age, it was a great show and I'm still not sure how he did it. My brother used to deliver papers to the Brush home in the early '70s, and he remembers seeing Serrano there all the time."

Rudy Gartner, an HB traffic parking control officer, also remembers stopping by to see Serrano. "They had a big sign on the barn that advertised Serrano—the World's Most Educated Horse. As I remember, the property stretched over about to where Norm's Restaurant is today."

Today, there is a Brush Drive just a block behind here where the Brush home (and Serrano) used to stand, which I believe is named for the family (though I am still researching to verify).

Serrano died in the early 1970s, and soon after, the property was torn down and Heil was widened. According to Hoxie, the Brush family owned another stable area at the southwest corner of Heil and Newland, but Serrano's primary residence was at the Beach Boulevard property.

Serrano was from the golden age of whimsical attractions that kept carnival barkers in business, an "Einstein Equine," as he was referred to, whose secret powers were never formally revealed. He was also a local HB resident that entertained kids who would stop by the Brush home to bask in the glow of the powers of the "Educated Horse."

So next time you pass the intersection at Beach and Heil, perhaps pause for a moment in honor of Serrano's former digs—a barn where magic, wonder and a bit of sideshow sparkle charmed old and young alike.

Chapter 4
Locals

LEROY

There are many palm trees in Huntington Beach, but few are as meaningful as the pair of graceful and slender Mexican fan palms that scrape the sky just several blocks from the ocean on Eighth Street. Like the house they sway in front of, they date back to the early 1920s.

What makes them so special? They were planted by a father to honor the day his son was born—an effort to create two lasting monuments to mark his baby boy's entry to this world. That proud papa obviously knew what he was doing because today the trees tower over everything in sight. That little boy, Leroy Jauman, is still thriving too. When Leroy's son, Jim, told me recently about his dad and the trees, I wanted to arrange a meeting at the house, which, incidentally, is also where Leroy was born in 1924.

Today, almost eighty-nine, he lives in Lakewood with his wife of sixty-one years, Yvonne, but Leroy's memories of old-time Huntington Beach are as sharp and vivid as the bright green fronds that grow in his honor atop the thin trunks.

Looking down the block at the structure that was once the Evangeline Hotel, Jauman fondly recalled visits he would make to the behemoth building. "The roughnecks from the oil fields stayed there," he told me. "And I'd bring bouquets of sweet pea flowers from my backyard to the lady that ran the place so she could decorate the dinner tables for them."

Leroy Jauman poses next to the house when he was born, in front of which stand the special palm trees.

For that, he'd pocket fifteen cents—a Depression-era bounty for an eight-year-old.

Kery Beason, who lives in Jauman's house today with her children, kindly let us visit in the backyard, where we compared a vintage image of the same spot. Jauman showed us where the sweet peas once flourished, next to where he grew black grapes in a small orchard.

Then he regaled us with memories of fearlessly climbing oil derrick towers with his friends, wandering the vast vacant lots and catching soft-shell crabs near the pier. They could fetch ten cents a dozen for the crabs during the Depression, and then the youths would spend the day jumping off the pier, which was allowed back then until an inexperienced "flatlander," as Jauman called him, was injured and his family sued the city. The kids also spent many hours riding the heavy wooden "belly boards" they made in shop class at Huntington Beach High School.

Several days later, I had the privilege of joining Jauman and a handful of his high school classmates, HBHS class of '42, who meet regularly at a local Marie Callender's. "Our group is shrinking," he said bittersweetly, showing me a contact list with many crossed-off names. But it doesn't dull the laughs and reminiscing that take place around the table.

Along with Jauman, Ray Walker, Cliff Clemens, Joanne Moore, Jean Parent and Rosemary Robinson all shared evocative local stories from the past.

"We had a war going on when we graduated," said Walker. "We didn't worry about college."

"Our generation had to grow up quickly," added Clemens. "Within a year, we were facing the enemy." All the men at the table enlisted. Clemens was held as a prisoner of war in a German camp.

They told me how military personnel in Huntington Beach back then were revered. Meals were provided, rides were given and over-the-top appreciation was the norm. "A serviceman wouldn't have to stand five minutes on the street before being offered whatever he might need," said Walker.

The group talked about long-gone neighborhoods and businesses, like the Green Shack, a down-and-dirty burger joint on the outskirts of town past the high school near the old tile factory where oil workers would frequent. They remembered dancing at the Golden Bear in the 1940s and then doing the "Balboa" dance at the Pavalon Ballroom adjacent to the pier, where famed composer and conductor Stan Kenton would sometimes perform (along with a local orchestra, the Esquires).

And they reminisced about lazy days swimming in the sea after sunning on the old wooden pier. Did you know that back in the 1940s, a shuttle boat from the pier would putter out about a mile offshore to a barge where you could sit and fish all day? It cost fifty cents round trip, and Clemens said that if you left early enough in the morning, by noon you had all the fish you could have wished for.

The boys all remembered the gun clubs too—twenty-three of them between Pacific Coast Highway and Westminster Boulevard. In fact, during duck season, they'd hop the Pacific Electric Red Car to the beach near the Bolsa Chica Gun Club before high school. They knew that at 7:00 a.m. sharp, the first barrage from the hunters would commence, sending the ducks in a flying scramble toward the ocean, where they'd float on the water until things quieted down. The kids, with shotguns of their own and hiding under tarps, timed things so they could blaze away from the beach and each get three or four ducks before class.

Can you even imagine?

By the way, while visiting Jauman's old home, his wife asked him if he'd told me about "the movie." I asked what she referred to and was informed of a film that was made in Huntington Beach in the 1930s, shot by a schoolteacher and actually starring Jauman and his classmates.

At the luncheon I attended, Rosemary Robinson brought along a copy for me to view. It is quite special.

Meantime, if you're ever on Eighth Street near Pecan Avenue and happen to notice those two palms, stare up high and consider what they represent. They are not just any trees, you know. They are a lasting gesture of love, a proud new father's way of saying, "Welcome, my son. To this world. To this family. To this town."

BILL KETTLER

I ran into my friend Marinka Horack recently at the Bolsa Chica Wetlands. She and her fantastic Miracle of the Marsh docent team from the Bolsa Chica Land Trust were taking yet another school group out to learn about nature. Marinka introduced me to an older gentleman, a docent, and said, "You should write about him, Chris."

I went back a week later to watch him teach the kids about birds and local history—as he told them, he'd actually been inside the Bolsa Chica Gun Club. In fact, this seasoned old sage even had a local elementary school named after him. So I took Marinka's advice.

A few days later, on a bright, warm day, we met at the end of Bolsa Chica Street, right where the Brightwater Trail starts (next to a six-acre parcel of land called the Goodell property). It was myself, my son and eighty-eight-year-old, lifelong Huntington Beach resident Bill Kettler.

Strong spring winds shook the palms and created waves in the carpets of vibrant yellow coast sunflowers. The view of the ocean was glorious from up on the mesa. But Kettler wasn't studying the view; he was ambling toward a cut in the fence, narrating his memory at this very same spot about seventy-five years ago.

"There were no houses out there; it was all rural," he said. "Far as you could see. I graduated from Springdale Elementary as class valedictorian—though there were only two of us in the class." With a short chuckle, Kettler motioned down at the soft dirt, which was studded with seashell fragments.

"These shells are all part of the Indian middens; their garbage heaps. This is where they discarded all their shells. I'd come up here as a young boy after the rains and look for arrowheads."

We kept moving ahead as Kettler looked for a special spot. "Things have grown over a lot, changed over the years," he said to himself. Then he

Bill Kettler standing at the precise spot where he found some very notable bones as a young boy back in the 1930s.

stopped at a point next to the thick, towering wild mustard. "It was here, right in here," he said softly. Kettler has led us to the exact site where, as a young teen in the early 1930s, he made a discovery. "I saw something shiny," he said. "Got closer and saw it was a skull. Then I saw another."

The rain had uncovered two complete ancient Indian skeletons, most likely at least several thousands of years old. He knew, after witnessing several scientific exhumations in the area, that he'd come upon part of a burial site. "I recognized the way the bodies were in a crouched position. No doubt in my mind. I collected them, every bone, and put them in a gunnysack to keep in my house. They were with the arrowheads and cog stones I'd discovered."

But years later, in the 1940s, an Apache friend told him that he needed to bury the skeletons with dignity.

"I was a horizontal engineer at that point in life," he laughed slyly. Huh? "I worked as a mortician. So I knew all the cemeteries in town. And I went over to Talbert and Beach and explained everything."

Today, in unmarked graves at Good Shepherd Cemetery, lie the two skeletons Kettler discovered. But that was not the end of them. In the early 1990s, when there was a proposal to build abut 4,800 homes at this site, Kettler said the developers told members of the Gabrielino-Tongva Band of

Mission Indians that the area was not all that sacred. An alarm went off in Kettler's head. He knew what the area held. So he told everyone what he'd found years ago.

Soon, hundreds of skeletons were found, and today, within view of where Kettler discovered his skeletons, we now have one of the most significant archaeological sites in Southern California. Known as ORA-83, this site contains evidence of an eight-thousand-year-old village and burial ground. It's also been the site of a long-running battle between Native Americans and developers over the right to build homes on hallowed ground.

Does Kettler realize his discoveries probably helped thwart the building of 4,800 homes on the mesa? "Well, I guess it didn't hurt," he chuckled. "And I mean, I hope it helped. We have to respect this history—how we can learn from it and also protect the legacy of the Indians and their families."

He served his country, he raised his family here, he had a school named after him and he never left his hometown. He also made a discovery, and looking at him on this picture-perfect day, it's easy to imagine how fired up a young boy's imagination was as he roamed this very site all those years ago.

He loved history, he loved exploring and he loved Indians.

Today, as he followed his own boyhood footsteps across the path, he wore a mischievous smile. I wonder what he was remembering.

A TEACHER IN THE WOODS

I'm standing in a glowing green meadow in the shadow of the El Capitan rock formation at Yosemite National Park on a warm spring afternoon. Nearby, my son Charlie and his eighth-grade classmates from Mesa View Middle School gawk at the nearby hulking figure. At first they're intimidated as he paws the air and gestures toward the sky. But they break into smiles when he approaches and playfully tousles a kid's hair.

It's not a bear but, rather, a lion of a man, science teacher Jay DuVal, who for thirty-five years has led students on a pilgrimage to what he considers a sacred place—a hallowed teaching sanctuary.

The former Iowa farm boy has taught in Huntington Beach since 1963, starting at Mesa View in 1993. The five-day Yosemite trips started thirty-five years ago when he and colleagues Rod Collier and Jim Henderson first dreamed up the idea (DuVal calls Collier the "father of the program"). Since

Teacher Jay DuVal teaching a group for students at Yosemite.

then, programs have sprouted at other schools, but DuVal's is thought of by many as not just the first but also the best. This, thanks to DuVal's creativity, energy and dedication to education.

About half the class (approximately 150 kids) takes the trip each spring, earning incentive points during the year to choose the hikes they want most (they can rack up points, for instance, working at a car wash and volunteering at the marathon, events DuVal also leads).

Premium hikes include Yosemite Falls and the Nevada Falls Loop, but Vernal Falls and Mariposa Grove are also popular, along with other activities. Nightly hikes and presentations fill out the week.

We arrive Monday at the historic Camp Curry, where kids will bunk four to a cabin. DuVal drops his bags and announces dramatically, "I am home." And with that, the week kicks off.

DuVal, along with veteran teacher/helpers Mike Merz, Craig Sears and Dennis Masuda, seems almost as giddy and mischievous as the kids. The stamina of the teachers belies their ages, and younger teachers (who will tackle the most strenuous hikes) pay close attention. After all, someday they will be charged with running the operation. For now, though, it's DuVal's show as he barks orders and gives direction with military gusto.

Each night, three groups rotate hikes with three teachers. Night one, we walk with DuVal, following a woodsy trail as pink shafts of light fade into the towering granite cliffs near the base of Yosemite Falls. The group of about fifty students hushes as, over the rush of the nearby water, Duval opens up about his first trip here. It was some thirty-five years ago. His dad had recently been killed in a farming accident back in Iowa. "I had lost my best friend, and my life had no meaning. One night, here in a meadow I sat. And thought. And found meaning again," he said.

His words hang heavy at dusk in the cool waterfall mist. As if paying tribute to his dad, he becomes a father figure in this setting, returning each year with the kids. He formulates the learning program, recruits teachers and parental chaperones and designs the activities. But it's his personality that steers the ship throughout the week.

One part Patton, one part Pied Piper, he trudges through the forests orating on Indian spirits, faith, hope, struggle and sacrifice. He implores the kids to "open their hearts" so they may learn about themselves. He commands and demands discipline, respect and decency—and he gets it. He builds character by barking, teasing, complimenting and comforting—sometimes all in one moment. He seems to know every leaf, every bird and every bit of bark. He shares his stories, folklore, theories, outrageous puns—and ire if the kids stray from the course.

The year's science lessons (among other courses) are all relived here in the natural world. DuVal constantly drills the troops with pop quizzes and memory testers, and they love it (especially when he rewards with small treats). If a kid gives up a seat to the elderly on a shuttle, they are introduced and applauded before dinner. Nightly grades are also given. "We got a B today," DuVal bellows, as if somewhere in the woods a tribunal is judging. "We need to get that up."

Later that evening, a group of teens lies on a bridge meditating, staring at the sky as a river rushes below. Jupiter appears as a white diamond over the ridge against a deep purple sky.

Cradled by nature, the kids ponder and dream, devoid (for the most part) of handheld electronics, music or TV. This is beautiful learning.

I hiked Nevada Falls with my son's group one day and was back on the ground with DuVal the next. Marching his kids through the forest, he identifies black oak, yellow pine and red-winged blackbirds. His voice cracks like thunder in the air. Then, under his breath, he tells me, "We teachers may be forgotten when we leave, but we live on through these kids."

Case in point: my bunkmate, Andy Arledge, whose daughter Carlee is on the trip, was a DuVal student about thirty-five years ago. An admitted handful as a youngster, Arledge said DuVal hasn't changed a lick.

"He's affected a lot of kids' lives for the better. I was a tough kid, and he had plenty of heart-to-hearts with me. He teaches life lessons today just like back then." Arledge is a captain and twenty-seven-year veteran of the Huntington Beach Fire Department. DuVal could not be more proud of him—and a bond remains. At a nightly chaperone meeting, it seems someone may have to tackle the grueling Yosemite Falls hike on back-to-back days. DuVal looks over to Arledge. "Anything you need, Jay. I'm here for you," the former student reassures. Chaperone Gayle Exton, another former student here with her daughter Chelsea, actually made two of the Yosemite trips years ago. Once a DuVal student, always a DuVal student.

The day before we leave, DuVal leads one last hike with his old buddy Craig Sears, who retires this year. This will be his last official trip, so DuVal lets him direct the trek.

Over lunch, DuVal tells the group how much Sears means to him, as a man and as a friend. "Of all the teachers I've ever worked with—he's number one."

There is deep affection between these two, who swap facts, old-guy insults and memories—lots of memories. And the teens love it.

We get back, have dinner and a final hike and then, too soon, it's over.

Friday morning, as our bus gently winds down the curving mountain road, many students snooze peacefully. Looking back from his front seat command perch, DuVal smiles as he surveys them, his eyes twinkling. Wistfully, he asks, "Don'tcha just love these kids?"

He may give me a detention for writing this, because he shuns credit, choosing instead to tout his team. But to you, Mr. DuVal, for the thousands of Huntington Beach students, parents and teachers whose lives you have enriched, we give thanks. You've demonstrated that teaching goes beyond a book, protractor or laptop. And you've magnificently leveraged the power of Yosemite to help our sons and daughters prepare for what lies ahead in that brave new world beyond eighth grade.

Photographer Ansel Adams said, "A true photograph need not be explained, nor can it be contained in words."

When Adams once greeted you and your students in a meadow, I wonder if he knew he could just as well have been describing you.

THE SINGING GOODTIMERS

It must be Wednesday morning at the Michael E. Rodgers Senior Center on Orange Avenue.

After all, even down the hallway from Room D, you can hear it. It doesn't matter that the door is slightly ajar; you'd hear it regardless. And outside the building on this clear, breezy spring morning, you'd hear it in the parking lot—maybe even out on the street.

There's no escaping it—the dulcet sounds of people singing from their hearts, loud and clear, with passion and exuberance. That's how the Singing Goodtimers do it, and that's a good thing.

Formed by vaudeville entertainer Esther Rivelli Brown back in 1971, today the group boasts about sixty seniors whose ages fall between the early sixties all the way up to ninety. They meet to rehearse each Wednesday in Room D for an hour, between 9:30 and 10:30 a.m., and a plaque outside the room acknowledges Brown, who died in 1998. It says, "Esther's charm and vitality will be missed. Her dedication to the seniors in Huntington Beach made a difference."

This is some more background from one of the coordinators of the group (and a lovely singer herself), Dianne Shirley: "Our singing group was formed in 1971 as a voluntary service organization, hopefully to bring pleasure to our community, especially our seniors. We entertain in senior community centers, retirement homes, convalescent hospitals, care homes and adult day-care centers. We are a voluntary service organization, and we are all seniors. We hope that we will inspire and encourage some of the seniors who listen to us to join in the fun, have a few chuckles and make life a little merrier. If we can encourage them to join us in singing, then we feel rewarded for our effort."

Wally Benton, a retired architect, has served as the group's conductor for several years. Acting as a sort of Fred Waring or Mitch Miller, he leads the group from the front of the room, stopping from time to time to clarify nuances in the songs.

Incredibly, every month the group's repertoire changes, swapping out twenty-five or so songs each time to reflect the theme of that particular month. For instance, January features show tunes, February is love songs, March is St. Patrick's music, April is light, spring songs and so on.

On this April day, I was treated to enchanting versions of "My Blue Heaven," "On a Clear Day," "Oh, What a Beautiful Morning," "Don't Sit Under the Apple Tree" and the closing showstopper, "I'm Forever Blowing Bubbles" (among many others).

Wally Benton leads the Singing Goodtimers at one of their rehearsals.

The old adage "They don't write 'em like that anymore" certainly applies to every Singing Goodtimers gig.

Chestnut after glorious chestnut has new life breathed into it by the group, many of whom actually grew up appreciating Tin Pan Alley classics in the era they were written. This is *Your Hit Parade* in the flesh, made possible by seniors who are not just donating their hearts but their souls as well.

The day I visited, about forty-five singers were there, prepping for a show the next day. Accompanied by piano and a few percussion pieces (and led heroically by Wally), they sang with the enthusiasm of teenagers meshed with an almost military precision. The joy in their faces seemed to signal that for all the happiness they bring to their audiences, there's something elixir-like in the magic of the music that makes the singers happy as well. Sure, it's logical to credit the Gershwins, Sammy Cahns and George M. Cohans of the world for writing such sturdy, dependable works of pop genius. And the Eddie Cantors, Judy Garlands and Nat King Coles for creating models of performance.

But give these seniors credit, too, because they seem to have found a fountain of youth in Room D—a space they've created that nourishes love, friendships and the celebration of the song. And they're using their talents to make others feel better.

When ninety-year-old Joe Splinggared stands to tackle one of the several solos that will be performed, the room gets extra still. I'm told Joe is battling Alzheimer's disease, but he'll never forget the songs. They're too ingrained in his psyche, evidently. In a soft tenor, Joe sings the standard "O Sole Mio." First in English, then in Italian—and it is exquisite.

What generations the Singing Goodtimers represent—of the Great Depression, world wars and victory gardens. Of big bands, jazz, bobbysoxers, Bogart, summer cotillions and Joe DiMaggio. Of hard work, discipline, decency—and generosity.

They are beautiful dreamers, one and all, and if I am allowed, I will return to Room D on occasion to listen, to watch and to bask in the glow of a very special group in this community.

I think they'd like the company if you'd ever like to pop in. And if you can sing, well, then you may never want to leave.

THE SILCOCK FAMILY

She looks reasonably relaxed and calm. She speaks in measured, thoughtful sentences, pausing from time to time to make sure she finds just the right word. A couple of her adopted pups trot in, two tiny hardship cases named Carl and Chad (the latter missing a leg—he was extra needy, and that's why he's here). She smiles a bit nervously as she says she'll be chaperoning her fifteen-year-old son's date later that afternoon. Just another day for a mom who has just helped get her twenty-nine kids ready for school.

Sharing a quiet moment with Ann Silcock is something to be valued and appreciated—she is a busy woman, after all. As you may be aware, Ann and her husband, Jim, have adopted forty-three children over the last ten years, focusing their life's energies on building a family made up of kids who, as Ann puts it, "people just didn't want. Kids who are disabled, abused...everything." But what may be cumbersome disabilities to some parents become diamonds in the rough for the Silcocks—they've watched boys bloom into young men in their household over the years, thriving in an environment that's nurturing, positive and productive.

The room where we sit is quiet and calm. We're in a house next door to their main residence, a place the Silcocks are adapting for their ever-growing brood. Next door, Jim is helping get the last kids off to school (currently, twenty-nine sons live at home, ranging in age from four to sixteen). This helps create some time for us to talk.

A stack of camp forms sits in front of Ann, and she'll pore over these after I leave. She says a typical day starts by setting the breakfast table for twenty-nine hungry mouths, followed by getting them off to school (twenty-eight will leave; one son is home schooled). At 2:00 p.m., the boys will start returning, and by 3:30 p.m., everyone is back home—at which point things like homework and recreational activities commence. Sixteen workers help with the boys who have total healthcare needs, and Ann and Jim use every free moment to forge special one-to-one relationships with each son, as well as provide a larger-scale family concept for the boys.

The main thing I want to know about today is a new musical CD put out by the family. Called *Team Silcock*, it is the second effort by the family and represents a therapeutic exercise in helping the kids think, dream and create.

Several years ago, Ann met singer/songwriter Dave Nachmanoff after he had played with Al Stewart at the nearby Coach House in San Juan Capistrano. A friendship developed, and soon, Ann had recruited Dave to bring his much-in-demand songwriting workshop right into the Silcock household.

Nachmanoff, a multi-talented writer/teacher/performer, was knocked out by the family. "Once I gained the confidence of the boys, it became easier to get them to open up as we created songs about their lives. The workshops we did were cathartic, and the songs have a real power to them. I was also impressed by this amazing notion of service the Silcocks have taught their sons. They're taught to help each other, to look out for each other—to care for each other."

Nachmanoff's deep connection with the kids resulted in *In the Family*, a seventeen-song CD featuring songs written by the Silcock family along with Nachmanoff. Now comes *Team Silcock*, featuring twenty new songs again written by the Silcock/Nachmanoff team.

Ann says the project was a wonderful chance to give the kids a vehicle for expression, as well as a lesson in the creative process. The lyrics read like diaries in a sense. From the title track: "Lots of brothers, they come from far and wide, Russian and Romania and also Oceanside. Carolina all the way to Kazakhstan brought together by the grace of a woman called St. Ann." And from "Family Sharing": "When you share you show respect. When you share, you're not just a little speck and people respect you too. When you share."

Plaintive and honest, the catchy, well-crafted songs (sung primarily by Nachmanoff with support vocals from the Silcock boys) are layered with lessons about the human experience. From "Enchantment Under the Sea": "At camp last summer, there in the gym, my heart was pounding, it was sink or swim. I was afraid. To take a risk…but if I didn't, what would I miss?"

A third CD is in the works, and Ann believes that with each new piece of work, their family's complex network will become simpler and stronger, and new bonds will be forged by working together and singing together.

VETERANS DAY

Sitting in a cozy Virginia living room on a crisp autumn afternoon, I could not be happier about who I am spending time with: Retired Rear Admiral Frank Gallo. He's my uncle, my godfather, and while I'm proud of him all the time, around Veterans Day the feeling crystallizes even more.

He still serves his country so faithfully and with such selflessness that I wanted to acknowledge his bravery. But with Veterans Day next week, I also wanted to let you know about some of the heroes with Huntington Beach roots.

Vi Cowden, a thirty-five-year Huntington Beach resident, describes herself as a former "little girl on the prairie." Originally from South Dakota, she dreamed of flying as long as she could remember. "I'd watch the hawks fly above the fields," she smiles, "and think, my God, if I could just do that."

In 1942, a local barnstormer taught Vi to fly, and the rest is history. World War II was declared, and she wanted to serve her country. There was no program for female fliers, so she contacted Washington to see what she could do to help. Soon, a program for female pilots opened, and Vi was on board.

Trained in Texas for the U.S. Air Force, she'd soon be picking up planes at the factory, taking them to training fields or places of demarcation— whatever helped the cause. She said she'd have loved to fly combat missions but was not allowed. Then the men came home after the war and wanted their jobs back, so Vi and her legion of other female fliers were deactivated.

"We didn't get our benefits for thirty-three years," she says. "But we survived and now feel we encouraged a lot of young women to take up flying. One thousand, seventy four of us made it through the training back then, and today many of us stay in touch."

Vi's favorite plane to fly was the P-51, the fastest plane then. "I was the first woman to deliver a P-51 to the Tuskegee Airmen," she said. "It went 445 [miles] per hour. One time when I took off, I thought, the quicker you got up, the better chance you had to survive. So I blast off once and a guy on the radio calls and says, 'Identify yourself.' I do, and he says, 'No woman can fly like that!'"

She still co-pilots from time to time, has been voted into various flight halls of fame and has been honored many times over for her skill and accomplishments. Incredibly, several years ago, she even went skydiving on her eighty-ninth birthday.

Vi Cowden poses with a picture of herself when she flew in the service.

Moving on from one interesting woman to another: Local Diane Gilliam now lives and works in Arizona as a civilian intelligence instructor. She joined the U.S. Army National Guard in 2000, and after a stint at the Fortieth Infantry Division at Los Alamitos training in army intelligence, she was sent to Afghanistan, where she interrogated Afghani prisoners. On November 23, 2003, the helicopter Gilliam and twelve others were traveling in suffered an engine failure. Five died in the horrific crash; Gilliam suffered multiple physical injuries and today experiences post-traumatic stress disorder.

But in talking to her, there are no regrets. She's a tough, funny young woman who manages to keep it all in perspective while focusing on the future.

Today from Fort Huachuca, where she teaches (she moved there in January), Gilliam says she wants to give back to a new generation and help them help their country. I know she makes her mom, Anita, proud—Diane, Surf City also salutes you.

Then there's Harold Tor, whom your kids might know. After all, for years he's been visiting local schools to talk about his life, and the kids love him. In 1944, the New Yorker faked his age to enlist in the army (he was just sixteen then).

He told me, "In Bensonhurst [New York], where I lived, there was a billboard that read, 'They serve their country.'

"On it, they had blue stars near the names of kids who were serving. In 1943, then into '44—the blue stars started turning into gold stars. That meant they were getting killed. Kids who played stickball in my neighborhood."

Former paratrooper Harold Tor at his home in Huntington Beach.

Soon, Harold was a paratrooper, and then he was off to New Guinea, the Philippines and the island of Luzon. In April 1945, General Douglas MacArthur declared the area secure and the campaign over. Three days later, Tor's squad was ordered to the Lake Taal area to inform Japanese troops that the war was over. But the Japanese answered with fire, and in the attack, Tor's hand was blown off.

After the war, Tor produced movies and appeared as an extra in about thirty films. He's a pilot, he's raced boats and today he and his wife, Donna, live in a beautiful home near the water.

A few years ago, Harold had a heart attack. Upon his return home from the hospital, he found seven hundred postcards from some students he had recently spoken to. He cried then, and recounting the story today, it still seems to get to him.

In 1954, President Eisenhower proclaimed November 11 as Veterans Day. In a letter, he said, "I have every confidence that our Nation will respond wholeheartedly in the appropriate observance of Veterans Day." And I hope everyone complies.

To these fine men and women I wrote about, and to all the others (including my uncle Fred DelGuidice, who served in the marines in World War II), thank you. We are indebted to you for your sacrifices.

ANOTHER VETERANS DAY

"That's the most beautiful thing—that flag." So whispered Helen Harris to me in her thick Greek accent as the Boy Scouts hoisted Old Glory on a warm, blustery day last Thursday, Veterans Day.

During World War II, Helen had been the official translator for the minister of foreign affairs in Greece.

She smiled into the sun as the wind caught the flag. Nearby, a woman in a wheelchair spontaneously started singing "You're a Grand Old Flag," bringing cheers and smiles from the assembled veterans and onlookers at Sunrise Senior Living in Huntington Beach (and Assisted Living and Memory Care community on Yorktown Avenue near city hall).

Jennifer Tremble, who is in charge of planning events for the facility, had invited me over, and I'm glad she did. I had not driven up to this property for more than ten years, not since researching the remains of the old Northam Ranch House for a book I was working on.

A warm, inviting place, Sunrise of Huntington Beach also happens to be home to many veterans.

There's former World War I navy man Joe Goss, who enlisted when he was seventeen. Glen Church enlisted at fourteen, but when the navy found out, they gave him the boot and told him to come back after school. So he did.

There's Watson Groce, another navy vet. He served in two wars and also enlisted at seventeen years of age. Jack Hardacre served in the air force and was stationed in Alaska for four years.

And the list goes on.

George Karabedian served in the navy, along with Edward Bryen, Donald "Whitie" Stanforth, Helen Johnson and Donald Braid.

Thomas Blake was in the air force for twenty years. Hy Tekler joined the army at nineteen, and Paul Taylor joined the marines at seventeen.

Looking at all of them today, identified with red, white and blue ribbon pins, it's interesting to imagine them as teenager soldiers—the same age as the kids across the street at Huntington Beach High School. But that's what they were—gutsy, brave, patriotic teenagers.

And they all live at Sunrise, quiet heroes one and all.

After the ceremony, the aforementioned Ms. Harris sat with me for a while to talk about her life. Clutching a small, worn photo album stuffed with pictures, notes and other shreds from a full, passionate life, she discussed her childhood in Constantinople and her husband, who passed away recently. She spoke of her two sons and her grandchildren.

And her life before the Communists took everything. "Not so bad though," she said. "Because it was after that we came to America. The most incredible place. The place that saved our lives after the war."

Helen was a gifted athlete, winning medals for Greece in several track events; she showed me the pictures. The striking, raven-haired young woman in the black-and-white images was gifted in another area too: language.

Helen Harris holds a picture of herself from back when she was approached by Adolf Hitler.

She became fluent in five languages (Greek, Polish, German, English and French), which made her invaluable as a translator.

Leaning over to speak in a whisper, she told me about an incident that happened during the war. "I was in Germany," she said, "and I was introduced to Adolph Hitler. Very strange moment. He told me I spoke perfect German, and he asked me how this was so, given that I was from Greece. I explained to him that I had a German nanny when I was young and that I picked it up from her."

Her eyes open wide and she shrugs as if to say, "What was I to do?" "He saw me in Poland once as well," she continued. "And remembered me. Came right over to say hello."

Also an expert in accounting, for twenty-seven years Helen worked at Bank of America in California.

Helen's old-world demeanor and experiences seem exotic today, because they are. But she is tied together with many other seniors at Sunrise for making a difference during wartime.

George Washington said, "The willingness with which our young people are likely to serve in any war, no matter how justified, shall be directly proportional to how they perceive the Veterans of earlier wars were treated and appreciated by their nation."

For all the veterans at Sunrise, and throughout Huntington Beach, we appreciate you and salute all that you have done for us and for this country. May every day be Veterans Day in the sense that the appreciation and gratitude we in the community feel never wanes or wanders.

Every Picture Tells a Story

On the car radio in a parking lot off Edinger Avenue near Edwards, Rod Stewart was singing "Every Picture Tells a Story." So it seemed fitting to investigate the history of a mural I've seen many times in the eleven years we've lived in Huntington Beach.

It covers a large wall facing the McDonald's that's located next to George's (a very good place for Mexican food). Have you seen it? It depicts all the most iconic McDonald's characters, from Ronald to Grimace to the Hamburglar, all hanging out in Huntington Beach.

The detail of the mural always interested me because of how accurate little touches are, like the old wooden HB sign that used to be located near the pier. Recently, I examined the signature in the painting's upper left border: "Danosian '92."

A bit of research revealed the following bio: "Saeed Danosian (Born November 1 1954, Tehran, Iran) was a contemporary Iranian artist, scholar and philanthropist based in Orange County, California.

For years, Huntington Beach locals had grown accustomed to seeing this mural painted by Saeed Danosian.

This rare photo shows the artist Saeed Danosian at work on the original mural.

"He pursued a program in interior design at the Bel Art Academy in Rome in the mid-70's, and from 1979 to 1985 studied further at the Academy of Fine Arts Vienna, earning his baccalaureate degree in set design for the theater in 1983 and his master's degree in set design and art direction in 1985. In addition to his areas of major concentration, his studies included film and television, costume design, art history, and music. He worked in the area of set design at both the Burgtheater and Wiener Staatsoper (Vienna State Opera).

"He died in Irvine, California on December 21, 2008 at the age of 54 from a sudden aortic dissection. He is buried in Pacific View Memorial Park in Corona del Mar, California."

Could this fascinating man have been the one who painted the mural? As it turned out, yes. Over the next several weeks, I was able to track down his wife, Yeganeh. I asked her about her husband, and her words were so eloquent and heartfelt that I'd like to present them here, essentially unedited. After reading them, you may never look at the mural the same way again. I know I won't.

My husband and I studied in Vienna, Austria. In 1979, while he was an art student at the Vienna Art Academy, he started working at

McDonald's as a manager. We were married very young, and he had to support me and later my daughter, who was born in 1980. We decided to move to America after we graduated. We came straight to Orange County in 1987 from Vienna. Our first language was Farsi and our second language was German, so we couldn't speak English well. With a master's degree in set design and art direction, he tried to find a job in his field, but he couldn't find anything, so because he had to support his family and he had experience from working as a manager in Vienna, he looked for a job with McDonald's Corporation.

Soon he found a management position at the Huntington Beach location while also teaching private art classes on the side. The owner learned about his background and how much he loved teaching kids about art, so when Saeed offered to create a painting on the wall for their young customers, they liked his sketch and they told him instead of working in the store, why don't you paint the mural? After that, he created a number of murals around OC, including at Mission San Juan Capistrano. At the time the mural was created, our daughter was twelve, and she loved the Happy Meal toys at McDonald's. He wanted to bring Ronald McDonald and his gang to life—enjoying the landmarks of HB such as the boardwalk, the lifeguard tower, the well-known HB sign and, of course, the happy whale jumping out of the water in the background.

Saeed was a very kindhearted person and a great human being, and I'm not saying this because he was my husband. At his funeral, which was held on Christmas Eve, there were hundreds of people present and numerous speeches given about how much Saeed had touched their lives. Irvine's mayor, Beth Krom, said, "He was always willing to give, with no expectations of getting anything in return." He donated so much of his time and worked with so many nonprofit organizations. The last ten years he taught as a professor at Westwood College, and in 2008 (only six months before his death), he was selected as National Instructor of the Year. We have received so many letters from his students and their families saying how much Saeed changed their son's/daughter's life. My daughter and I are truly proud of him.

He loved Huntington Beach and especially the young community that resided there. He was so good at connecting with the younger generation and always interacted with the kids who were biking and skateboarding around HB.

There are countless memories I have of my husband. Every day with him was a day of happiness, positivity and laughter. When he walked into a room, he brightened it with his smile and energy. He had the biggest heart. After his death, Westwood College dedicated their student commons area to him because of the difference he made in their school. He truly was one in a million. To come here with nothing and leave behind such a lasting impression on so many people is so amazing.

I thank Yeganeh for telling us the story of the mural and her husband. It always struck me as a piece of art that was created with much love and laughter. And obviously, it was.

To hear the story of its creation by a man of deep talents and character breathes new life into a fading picture—a unique portrait of our city tucked away on the side of a building.

Rod Stewart was right.

EVERY PICTURE TELLS A STORY PART II

I wrote about a mural in this column two years go. It covered a large liquor store wall facing the McDonald's near the intersection of Edinger Avenue and Edwards Street, and it depicted all of the most iconic McDonald's characters, from Ronald to Grimace to the Hamburglar, all hanging out in Huntington Beach.

As I described back then, the detail of the mural interested me because of how accurate the little touches were, like the old wooden HB sign that used to be near the pier. After seeing an artist signature, "Danosians '92," I did some research.

I learned that Saeed Danosian had been born in Iran in 1954. An artist, scholar and philanthropist, sadly, he had died in Irvine back in 2008 from a heart ailment.

After tracking down his wife, Yeganeh, his rich story was revealed to me. Danosian had studied throughout Europe and, in Vienna, took a job at a local McDonald's. After moving to Orange County in 1987 with his wife and daughter, the artist took another job at this particular McDonald's in Huntington Beach while also giving art lessons. Soon after, Danosian painted the now-beloved mural on the wall adjacent to the restaurant.

Saeed loved Huntington Beach, and many of us loved his mural. Recently, the McDonald's was remodeled. One morning last month, I noticed a sizeable part of the mural was painted over with a beige patch. Were they just protecting it? I asked inside the liquor store, but they didn't know. Then last week, the day the restaurant reopened, the mural was completely gone, all painted over. It was like losing a friend.

After the mural was vandalized by a vegan group, the McDonald's adjacent to it decided to completely paint over the wall.

So what happened?

I called John Patterson, who has been the operation supervisor at the restaurant since 1992. He said that last month, during the renovation, the mural had been badly vandalized. "We were heartbroken when we came in the next morning and saw this. In twenty years, we had never had any graffiti vandals touch the mural," he told me.

That's what prompted the first patch. He said the mural was finally painted over because it could not have been saved. It was merely put out of its misery. However, he hopes they can create a community project to re-create the original. "I worked here with Saeed," he told me. "He was running shifts while he painted it. Then he came and touched it up later on. He was a very special and talented man. We want to re-create his legacy somehow on that wall. His work deserved better than what happened."

As for the vandals, as you can see from the photo on the next page that Patterson took, it was a group of vegans making a "statement." Never mind that their statement was at the expense of everyone else, that it ruined a precious piece of art and that it was flat-out vicious. Not to condemn all vegans, of course, but the militant fringe within any group needs to be called out for what they usually are: gutless, fly-by-night cowards. I saw similar

This is what the manager of the McDonald's arrived to discover one morning. No arrests were ever made for this case of vandalism.

cowardice this election season, with the surgical cutting out of messages from many signs posted in people's front yards and on street corners. Through their own militant Orwellian lenses, the fringe often believes their voices supersede all, public or private property be damned. If they disagree with your message, rather than reason, they destroy it. Case in point, this destruction.

I contacted Yeganeh to let her know what they had done to her husband's work. She was upset but is hopeful that it can be redone. She also graciously supplied some photographs of the work as it was being created by her husband, along with some original sketches.

In the meantime, to the vegan vandals who did this, trust me, not loving you at all right now.

Chapter 5

THE SPORTING LIFE

PLAY BALL!

Being one of the 115,300 baseball fans at the Coliseum as the Dodgers played the Red Sox last week was a memorable experience to be sure.

But for this Angels fan, it was simply a warm-up for what matters most: the home opener in Anaheim. As I write this column, game time looms, and so I will type fast—we like to get there in time to catch some batting practice.

This is my twelfth or so opening day watching a team I have grown to love. I came here a Mets fan from New York, but that mid-'90s squad won me over, and for my entire family, there has been no looking back. We simply love the Angels.

That's why it was such a pleasure speaking with Hank Conger last week. After all, Hank was raised here in Huntington Beach, his family still lives here and, as you may know, in 2006 the Angels picked him first in that year's draft. Since then, the former Huntington Beach High School catcher has been working hard to develop his game, and last week he was back home for a couple days.

Hank said he was about to return to Arizona for some rehab work before starting his season in earnest. He wasn't sure yet whether he'd be with the Cedar Rapids Kernels or the Rancho Cucamonga Quakes, but either way, he was anxious to get back behind the plate.

Conger had just arrived home after experiencing his first major-league training camp, and he recounted it with the zeal and enthusiasm not just of a young player but as a fan, as well.

Local catcher made good, Hank Conger.

"The guys were just amazing," Hank said. "Jeff Mathis and Mike Napoli gave me lots of time and tips in terms of catching. And I also got to work with Mike Scioscia, which was amazing."

Conger grew up an Angels fan, so the entire experience of actually being part of the Angels organization still seems a bit surreal for him.

"When I was a kid, I always followed Garret Anderson, [Darin] Erstad, Frankie Rodriguez and of course Tim Salmon. So having Tim come to camp this spring and talk to us about his love of the game, his passion for hitting—it was unbelievable," he said.

The kid who made his mark at Ocean View Little League still loves to come home when he gets the chance, both to catch up with his buddies and spend time with his family (Conger's younger brother, Adrian, plays baseball at Huntington Beach High School).

Hank's dad, Yun, is thrilled thus far with how the Angels organization has treated his son—and the entire family. "They are incredibly professional, just the best," Yun told me. "Owner Arte Moreno has been wonderful, the scouts; everyone has gone out of their way to make this a great experience for my son and for us too. The communication is very clear, and they really seem to care about their players. My wife, Eun, and I could not be happier."

And just what is Hank looking forward to this coming season? "Having fun, staying healthy and playing hard." Sounds good, Hank. You've got a good city rooting behind you, so go get 'em, and I'll do updates here "In the Pipeline" as your season progresses.

OK, almost time to leave for the game. Another Angels opening day. Another moment for local baseball fans to savor the arrival of our national pastime. Baseball Hall-of-Famer Rogers Hornsby once said, "People ask me what I do in winter when there's no baseball. I'll tell you what I do. I stare out the window and wait for spring." Well, with that first pitch, for me, spring will officially be here. So go Angels! (And go Hank Conger!)

HERE'S THE PITCH

The only thing better than spring baseball and summer baseball is, of course, autumn baseball, particularly if your team is in the playoffs.

My team, the Angels, are in. Paul Anderson, city editor for the *Independent*, is happy because his team, the Cubbies, is also in. I'm sure for many other locals here in Huntington Beach, the baseball bliss has begun as the red—Angels red, that is—is donned for the current divisional series.

Ian Kennedy, one of the many local athletes who has made it in professional sports.

Many locals will never begin to appreciate the good fortune of being a scant twenty minutes away from a beautiful ballpark where the temperature will probably not dip below seventy before any first pitch. Compare that with long, slow, bundled-up subway rides to East Coast games that can easily run past midnight, and you'll know we live in baseball heaven. As a former East Coaster, I'll take this any day, even with the Rally Monkey.

There's another reason to pay attention here in Huntington Beach as the playoffs commence—a former local youngster may factor big in this postseason. His name is Ian Kennedy, the former USC star pitcher who now wears Yankee pinstripes. I spoke with Kennedy last week, and he's excited about the prospect of perhaps pitching in the playoffs right here in Orange County before his family and friends.

Some background: Kennedy grew up in Huntington Beach and attended La Quinta High School in Westminster (other major-league alumni from La Quinta include Bobby Crosby, Gerald Laird and Ian Stewart). He went on to star at USC and then was drafted by the New York Yankees in the 2006 Major League Baseball Draft (first round, twenty-first pick overall). Kennedy pitched for the Staten Island Yankees of the New York–Penn League, the Class A Tampa Yankees of the Florida State League and the AA Trenton Thunder of the Eastern League. On July 24, Kennedy was promoted to the AAA Scranton/Wilkes Barre Yankees, and then just several weeks later, on September 1, he made his sparkling debut at Yankee Stadium in place of Mike Mussina. He got the win by allowing just one earned run and striking out six in just seven innings.

I asked him, what was it like to make your debut in perhaps the most hallowed of stadiums? "It was amazing," Kennedy told me from the locker room in the House That Ruth Built. "I don't know a whole lot about baseball history, but I know about that place, and it was unforgettable."

Was he nervous?

"Not really," Kennedy said. "I had Roger Clemens talking to me about how to be tough and handle the better hitters. Plus, Moose [Mussina] was real supportive, so I was in good hands."

To say the least.

Kennedy said his entire family was on hand and told what a thrill it was to see them after the game. He doesn't get back to Huntington Beach too much, so seeing friendly faces on the road is a good way to help settle you down.

He said he admired Greg Maddux the most while growing up, and though he hasn't had the chance to meet him yet, he's working on it.

"There's nobody like Maddux," the powerful righty says.

We also talked a little bit about baseball movies.

"I'd say my favorite is *The Sandlot*," he said. "It's an awesome movie because it's all about playing just for the love of the game. No money or nothing, just love of the game. "

Kennedy laughed when I asked what it would be like to try to secure tickets for everyone in Anaheim should the Yankees and Angels both advance to the league championships. "That's going to be crazy. For sure I'll have to see about getting some tickets off the other guys on the team."

One curveball Ian Kennedy may have to deal with is his wedding—scheduled for October 6 at Westborough Country Club in Kirkwood, Missouri. (His fiancée is Allison Jaskowiak, a USC basketball player.) Back when the date was set, he had no idea he'd be where he is, but Kennedy said he's sure they'll figure something out.

So by all means, root for the home team this postseason. But also root for the home player—Yankee star-on-the-rise (and Huntington Beach's own) Ian Kennedy.

GOLDEN GIRL

My mom, who also lives here in Huntington Beach, has always had a knack for meeting interesting people in unexpected places. So it was no surprise when she told me about her mail carrier, Shirley, and what a nice, helpful, friendly woman she was. However, what did manage to get my attention after hearing more about Shirley (and eventually meeting her) was that Shirley was not just any Shirley—she's Shirley Babashoff, eight-time Olympic medalist and one of the greatest swimmers in recorded history.

Surely you remember Shirley. In Montreal, she was the 1976 Olympic gold medalist in the 400-meter freestyle relay and silver medalist in the 200-meter, 400-meter and 800-meter freestyle and 400-meter medley relay. At Munich, in the 1972 Olympics, she won gold in the 400-meter freestyle relay and silver in the 100-meter and 200-meter freestyle. As well, she won the 1975 World Championship in both the 200- and 400-meter freestyle. She also won five additional world championship medals and twenty-seven national titles and set eleven world records in eight different events and twenty-nine American records in twenty-seven separate events.

Shirley Babashoff holds two of her medals from the 1972 and '76 Olympics.

Shirley was named 1974's USA Sportswoman of the Year and *Swimming World* magazine's American Swimmer of the Year in 1976, and when she retired, she was the all-time leader among U.S. women (a record she held for twenty-four years until Dara Torres and Jenny Thompson finally surpassed her career total in 2000). Plus, she was inducted into the International Swimming Hall of Fame in 1982 and U.S. Olympic Hall of Fame in 1987.

But for all the awards and accolades, for all the records and glory, there's something else that I think distinguishes Shirley Babashoff as an exceptional champion: she's the one who first had the guts to publicly flag and challenge the East Germans on the fact that they were pumping their swimmers with major doses of steroids—that they were turning the 1976 Olympics into a Frankenstein freak show.

Her hunches started developing back in 1973, when she noticed female East German swimmers developing higher muscle mass and lower voices. But then, at Montreal in 1976, when she and her teammates found themselves losing the gold to athletes who were clearly doped, Shirley had had enough. She gave a voice to what many were thinking but were too scared to address directly.

She called the East German squad on the carpet. What did she get for her troubles? The nickname "Surely Shirley," tagged as a sore sport by many in the international press and criticized for "only" winning a batch of silvers along with her one gold.

But time has been a friend to Babashoff because since then we have learned that the East Germans did in fact cheat the rest of the world's athletes. In 1976, East German swimmers won eleven of thirteen gold medals. This was after winning none in 1972. Do the math today and it would only seem right to strip them of their gold and place the medals where they rightfully belong: with American swimmers.

Though Shirley has made recent appeals to Olympic officials, it seems unlikely today that anything will ever be done about it. But thankfully, she has no regrets about what she did (today, in light of the many steroid scandals, her actions seem more timely than ever).

In conversation, Shirley Babashoff is still outspoken. She's also funny, honest and a terrific storyteller. She talks about what it was like to be a fifteen-year-old competing at Munich and how strange it was one day to find armed guards at the cafeteria, the day the terrorists attacked. How all the young female athletes, who first loved the privacy of having their own little studio apartments, then crammed into those apartments for safety and company.

She recounts meeting President Ford before the 1976 Olympics, the joys of competing, growing up in Whittier (her brother Jack was also an Olympic swimmer) and what her post-Olympic life has been like. She retired before the boycotted 1980 Olympics and, along with fellow Olympian multi-medalist Mark Spitz, became a spokeswoman for a swimsuit company. After that, she coached swimming for ten years. In 1986, she had a son, Adam. She raised him as a single parent, and today the bond between them seems profoundly strong.

And for twenty years, she's been a mail carrier here in Huntington Beach for the United States Postal Service.

She doesn't have a pool where she lives, but she still looks to hit the water whenever she can.

Cradling her gold and silver medals, she offers details of the awards: the silver is pure, the gold is plated and sometimes the chains on them break. They are priceless reminders of thousands of hours of training, countless travel miles and the grit and determination of a young Whittier girl who could outswim all the boys.

Perhaps someday the Olympic Committee will figure out a way to correct the blatant cheating that took place. It did award the Olympic Order to

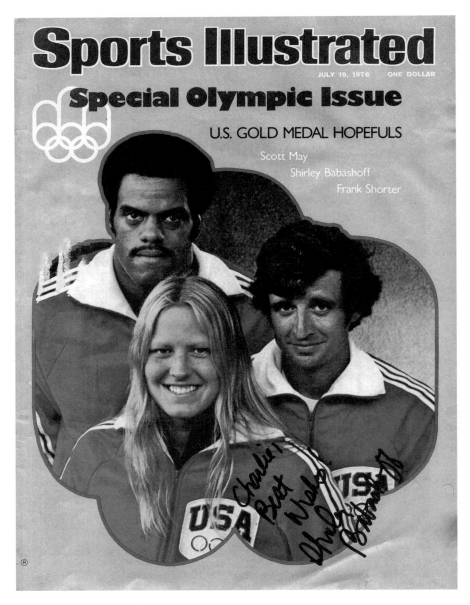

Shirley Babashoff on the cover of *Sports Illustrated* in 1976.

Shirley in 2005, an honor established in 1974 to acknowledge individuals who have "illustrated the Olympic ideals through actions, have achieved remarkable merit in the sporting world or have rendered outstanding services to the Olympic cause." Maybe the committee understands that she was the one who changed history by speaking out.

But regardless, if you live along Warner near Bolsa Chica, pay close attention to your mail carrier. It may just be Shirley Babashoff, a legendary American champion who didn't just have the talent to make a difference—she also had the guts.

What do you think? Should the Olympic medals be rightfully awarded to the American swimmers?

Disc Golf

This summer, we learned something new about Huntington Beach, thanks to one of our friends, Daniel Boucher. For his fifteenth birthday, Daniel wanted to play disc golf with some of his pals at Central Park.

My son Charlie and I were there to help celebrate, and we were anxious to try the golf too. Like so many other things, we've passed it a thousand times. We were intrigued but never took the time to stop and give it a try.

Not being a golfer, the concept of the sport never quite hooked me. However, driving past Central Park and seeing the odd blue, yellow, red or white disc soaring by did bring back enough childhood Frisbee memories to spark a bit of nostalgia. As I'd soon learn, my circa 1974 lime-green Wham-O would have no place on the course. And forget the word "Frisbee." These are "discs," dude.

Some background: The disc golf course in Huntington Beach is the second-oldest disc golf course in the world (the first is in Pasadena). Back in 1979, Tom Kennedy won $50,000 in a disc golf tournament played here that was broadcast for ABC's *Wide World of Sports*.

The rules of disc golf relate to golf, but instead of hitting a ball with a club, you throw discs toward a metal target basket, which features a web of chains designed to deaden the impact of the disc and catch it. Each hole on the eighteen-hole course has a determined par (three or four in Huntington Beach), and putters and drivers (differently shaped discs) are used in a similar manner to golf course play.

On the day we played with Daniel, it became clear this was not like throwing a regular Frisbee. The discs we rented were made of much harder plastic; they had sharper edges and could be downright dangerous in the wrong hands (on several holes, mine). Traversing the course, it was amazing to me how many hardcore disc golfers were out playing seriously—very seriously.

Armed with carrying bags that were sort of like large CD holders, golfers toted as many as two dozen discs each. For every hole, for every shot, for every course quirk—there was the right disc. Colorful discs were flying past at alarming speeds and distances, but "Fore" was usually called, and there was a laid-back atmosphere among the devoted that brought back memories of Grateful Dead concerts and Reggae Sunsplash shows. Once we got the semi-hang of how to achieve some distance and accuracy, the fun kicked in—along with the competition.

Jerry Davis runs the shop and course, and he's not just knowledgeable—he's a renowned disc golfer. "I started playing casually back in 1990, and my first actual round of disc golf took place at HB disc golf course," he said.

He started playing amateur tournaments in 1996 and was competing in professional events by 1999. He won his first pro-sanctioned event in Goleta/Santa Barbara at the 2001 Evergreen Open. "[I had] several top ten finishes and a fair share of bottom ten finishes, admittedly," he said.

As for our local course, David said, "It was designed by the late, great Ed Headrick in 1977. Huntington Beach has a long history of producing world-class disc golfers who are regularly ranked among the top twenty-five in the world. And here at the course, being able to rent discs and receive some free basic instruction makes this course attractive to new players. Most veteran disc golfers are more than willing to share tips with novice players. It's cheap and fun."

He's not kidding. Prices range from one dollar on weekdays to two dollars on weekends. (That's not a typo.) And drinks and snacks are available for less than two dollars. In terms of what you get, this may be the best dollar you ever spend in your life.

Robert McIntee has helped run the pro shop for the last several years. Now twenty-two, he's among the top forty disc golfers in the world.

"I first played in 2001," he told me. "I grew up playing regular golf with my grandfather, but once I tried this, I was hooked. It was so cheap to play; I could play all the time."

McIntee is sponsored today by Discraft, and he's traveled the world playing competitive disc golf, which both he and Jerry Davis believe should be an Olympic sport.

Charlie and I returned several times in the following weeks. We purchased our own discs and even made it over to play the course in La Mirada, which I liked but not as much as the Huntington Beach course.

One quiet weekday, we saw a burly, late twenty-ish guy tossing alone—practicing more than actually playing the course. His tosses were jaw dropping. The discs he threw seemed to explode off his steely arm, soaring missile-like for what looked to be about 150 to 175 yards. We asked him for a few tips, and he gratefully obliged.

This was John Gera, who quietly went about his business making mincemeat of the course—a born disc golfer but not one who likes organized competition. "I play for myself and not for anything else," he told me. "It is therapeutic for me. Some people take it very serious, and I do as well when there are things on the line. I have been playing for fourteen years. Started at twelve with my dad's neighbors and loved it ever since. My dad played in Huntington Beach in the late '70s, and he took me out in a stroller in '84, so I guess it's kind of ironic that two decades later I'm doing the same thing with my daughter."

And his tips for beginners? "Just take your time and let the disc do the work—not you. Take your time and always have fun, because if you're not having fun, what is the point?"

Gera seems to have the sort of Zen approach (as do Davis and McIntee) that makes for a great disc golfer.

But there is a huge range of players on the course most days, from first-timers to weekday hackers to polished pros. Everyone seems to get along, it's laid-back and, again, it's an unrivaled bargain. There are lots of free help and tips available and amateur leagues—an entire disc golf sub-culture that is thoroughly cool and enjoyable.

I admit being very late to this game after living here almost ten years, so thanks are in order to Daniel.

DOROTHY

The three-time French Open finalist moves fluidly across the tennis court, setting her opponent up with a well-disguised drop shot and then finishing the point with a cross court overhead. I am not watching the Tennis Channel nor am I seated in the grandstand at Roland Garros near Paris, France, where the French Open is currently in full swing. Rather, I am at a local tennis center watching a legend do what she's done for nearly seventy years: play tennis with grace, energy and smarts. Lots of smarts. Her name is Dorothy Knode, she's eighty-one years old and she lives right here in Huntington Beach.

Dorothy Knode poses on the local tennis court.

It's a wonderful time for local sports right now, what with the Angels and especially the Ducks playing so well. But for tennis fans (of which I am a huge one), the French Open presents a unique, seductive appeal. Sliding across the slow, unpredictable, red brick–colored clay, players seem more dramatic, more warrior-like. Dorothy knows the feeling well. She was (and is) a clay court specialist with a particular fondness for the French. After all, Knode reached the women's singles final of the French Championships in 1955 and came within two points of owning the crown (she lost to Angela Mortimer Barrett 2–6, 7–5, 10–8). In 1957, she made it back to the finals and lost to Shirley Bloomer Brasher (6–1, 6–3). In 1956, she and her partner, Darlene Hard, were the runners-up in the French Open's doubles championships, losing to the team of Althea Gibson and Angela Buxton.

From 1952 through 1957, Knode reached the semifinals of six other Grand Slam singles tournaments and also racked up plenty of titles: the singles winner at the German Championships in 1950, 1952 and 1953; singles title at the U.S. Clay Court Championships in 1951, 1955, 1958 and 1960; and the bronze medal at the 1959 Pan American Games in Chicago. And it goes on.

We first met at her home as she was preparing for a weekend garage sale. My son and I helped her organize some items, sifting through old trophies, certificates and other evidence of a successful, globetrotting tennis life. Still energetic and wonderfully chatty, Knode's eyes light up as she describes playing in the City of Light before the existence of million-dollar contracts and endorsements or guarantees (interestingly, celebrities back then would sometimes sponsor a favorite player to help pay for travel, equipment, etc.). "I loved the people, the food, the wine—it was a wonderful era to be in Paris." She recounts the then-exotic travel, her friendship with the legendary Althea Gibson and how close she came to that French title. "I was serving for the match and the score was 30–15. Just two points away—oh well—it just wasn't meant to be, I guess."

On her wall are old photos that reveal how much tennis styles have changed since the 1950s, before the game's elegance and formality gave way to neon-colored costumes and space-age racquets. But you won't find Dorothy bemoaning

Dorothy Knode with one of her many trophies in her Huntington Beach home.

the current state of tennis. Hardly. "I really enjoy following Roger Federer, James Blake and Maria Sharapova, among some others," she says in her musical, lilting voice. "Of course, I wish we could have made their money, but it was a different time, and we did incredibly interesting things and met wonderful people."

And Dorothy Knode doesn't just enjoy watching the game today—she is still an active participant in international and national senior events and still manages to play for fun several times a week. (She won the eighty-and-over Super-Seniors World Individual Championships in Antalya, Turkey, in 2005 and leaves to play in a tournament in Forest Hills, New York, in just a few weeks.)

Watching her run a delicate finger over a big, old, unpolished singles trophy, one senses that she relishes those glory days. And why not? For a California girl back then to be playing at Wimbledon, Paris, Egypt and many other far-off corners of the globe had to be heady stuff. A yellowed, illustrated poster on her wall features her pretty, smiling, twenty-four-year-old face—and her star quality is evident.

But as tempting as it might be to sit and relive the past, that's not Dorothy's game. She still has a career, after all, and watching her play today, it's evident how competitive and crafty her style is. Her game face is on as she moves the younger player around the court, dispensing with occasional bits of advice but always looking for the win. After playing for about ninety minutes, she puts the last shot away. Packing her bag up at courtside, she smiles and tells her opponent he needs to be quicker to get to the net when she deposits one of her patented drop shots over. But I can tell you, as someone who watches (and plays) a lot of tennis, some of those shots were just too good, no matter how quick the opponent.

This weekend, when the finals of the French Open are on, Dorothy Knode will be watching at home in Huntington Beach. And she'll know what the players are going through, because she's been there.

THE BOYS OF SUMMER

When I first spoke to Ocean View Little League manager Jeff Pratto, it was hard to hear him. As he explained over the noise behind him, he and the team had just arrived in Williamsport, Pennsylvania, hallowed home to the Little League World Series, and were about to take part in a parade featuring all the teams from around the world that had earned their place in the sun (or, as it turned out, some rain too).

Such was the continued dream-like trail for the Surf City Boys of Summer, a poised, disciplined group of young players that, under Pratto and his equally poised and disciplined coaching staff, found themselves sitting on the cusp of that rarest of baseball achievement: a World Series Championship.

I remember playing in Little League All Stars back in the early 1970s. We'd won a couple games, and all of a sudden, all we had to do was win about fifteen more to make it to Williamsport. That never happened, but following this team today is a wonderful reminder of the power of the game and the strangely beautiful sound of dreams coming true.

Have you been following them? Last Sunday, the Ocean View Little League, representing the West Region, beat La Grange, Kentucky, 10–0. Two days earlier, they had defeated Rhode Island 11–0. Twenty-one runs, and not one home run. Rather, they relied on key hitting and great pitching, the hallmarks of most great teams.

I spoke with Pratto after the first game, and he did not seem too shocked at the outcome. "I expected we'd win," he said, "but never did I imagine an 11–0 victory. I just have great faith in these kids and their abilities. I mean, our top four guys had just two hits between them—so that says a lot about the depth and determination of this team."

I was curious how the kids were dealing with the pressure of the environment—the throngs of fans, the ESPN coverage—was it having an effect at all?

"Not really. As far as ESPN goes, the only real effect they have is we can't leave the dugout until they say go, when the broadcast starts. That's no big deal. The game really remains the same as it is back home in Huntington Beach. Except for the rain delay—we don't get a lot of that back home."

Pratto (who said this series will be the end of his managing career) told me that the organizers take special care to shield the players from too many distractions. "They're great," he said. "They keep us locked down pretty good. Security is good. We get to practice normally and go to the batting cages and all. The kids really are having fun. There are no assigned tables for eating, so they're getting to meet kids from all over the world. And in the dorm, we're right next to the Canadian team. It's an awesome experience for these kids. I mean, there were forty-two thousand people at the game yesterday—a new record. Talk about the memories these kids will have."

As for Pratto's son Nick, after this series he'll be heading up to Cooperstown, New York, to play in another tournament, then it's down to North Carolina to try out for Team USA. But for now, all focus is on the series in Williamsport.

After Sunday's 10–0 rout against Kentucky, I spoke to Pratto again, and he conveyed that the kids are not getting overconfident—not even close to it. "Part of what I preach is cautious optimism and that we'll take things one day at a time. But these kids are pretty savvy at this point and very businesslike. For them, it's just about getting the next game, no big jumping around or celebrating or anything. Just being calm and cool. Our next opponent, Montana, is undefeated, so we know what we're up against. What happens will happen, but our goal is to be America's best—that's what's on the players' minds as well."

Before ending our conversation, Pratto wondered, "Are people back home interested in this?" I assured him many are.

"Good," he said. "These kids deserve the attention. They're really playing their hearts out."

THE BOYS OF SUMMER II

As I write this, it is early Sunday morning, several hours before Ocean View Little League's championship World Series game versus Japan (an interesting coincidence, given that one of our sister cities is located in Japan). The teams, of course, are about 2,600 miles east in Williamsport, Pennsylvania.

I'm here in Huntington Beach, sitting by Ocean View's home field, part of Murdy Park. State senator John A. Murdy donated the fifteen-acre parcel of land for this park in 1962. The skate park here is the first skating facility ever constructed in Orange County. This is also the location of the very first community center ever built in Huntington Beach.

But from now on, the park will probably be best known for this team.

And I'm thinking as I write this that no matter what happens in the championship game, we should all remember this field, and tell people about this field, and celebrate the young men who play baseball on this field. Because regardless of the final score today, what the Ocean View Little League team did in the last several weeks was quite extraordinary. In fact, what all the teams did (and do each season in Williamsport) is extraordinary.

They leave their small towns, their big cities and their far-off countries to play on a world stage. All of a sudden, tens of thousands of people flock to see them, to cheer them and to revel in their accomplishments. They compete with the most elite players from around the globe, all the while representing, in near-Olympic fashion, where they come from. Babe Ruth once said, "I won't be happy until we have every boy in America between the ages of six and sixteen wearing a glove and swinging a bat." And so somewhere, Babe Ruth must be smiling.

As I write this, the sprinklers have just shut off, and home plate sits in a muddy, sandy pool. And it is all but silent. An already-warm breeze moves some infield dirt, but there is no baseball here today. Yet something hangs in the air, some far-off echo of aluminum bat meeting ball, the smack of a ball meeting glove, the long-ago cheers of families on a balmy evening. If you listen closely, you might hear an umpire's bellow, or an upbeat "2-4-6-8" cheer, the winner's cheer, along with a less hearty chant from the losing side.

I came here to quietly honor this team before the game because win or lose in the final, what they have already done, for me, almost renders the last game anticlimactic.

Any Google News search of Huntington Beach in the last year or two has produced a slew of negative news stories related to our city. Escalated drunk driving statistics, a hotel that caters to sex offenders, downtown boozing and

The baseball diamond at Murdy Park, home of the 2011 World Series champions, Ocean View Little League.

brawling, the Robert Rizzo affair and more ugly episodes that don't just leave dents in a city—they leave big, ugly scars.

And along comes this group of disciplined, composed, poised players (and coaches and parents) to rewrite the headlines. After eliminating team after team with an almost businesslike expertise out here, they headed back east to the hallowed fields at Williamsport. While there, they made friends with other teams, they rode in a parade and game by game they won the hearts of millions of Americans. They exemplified the spirit of the game and were sportsmanlike and hardworking and behaved with class. They laughed and played like the kids they are, and they will no doubt return with a ballpark full of memories.

However, they also helped restore this city's image as a place with solid, decent, hardworking people who play hard but by the rules. They put Huntington Beach back on the map for all the right reasons.

As well, they didn't just make this city proud, they made this country proud and in turn also reminded many of us why we fell in love with this game in the first place, many of us as Little Leaguers ourselves. I received many notes this past week from readers expressing that they were enjoying the Ocean View game as much or even more than Major League games.

Why? Because it was real. There was not a penny involved. Even tickets to the games were all free. As heavy as the cliché sounds, this really is playing for the love of the game. Because that's all these kids know right now—this marvelous game that connects generations and bridges international gaps and elevates that most simple act, having a catch, into an almost religious exchange of simple glory and connection.

Speaking with manager Jeff Pratto the last couple of weeks gave me some nice insight into this team and its approach. His calm, steady demeanor clearly influenced his team, so he should be applauded. As of this moment, his team is the best in the country. By the end of the day, they may be crowned the best in the world. But as he told me, their goal was a U.S. title. And they achieved that.

Sitting here by their field of dreams, I take one last look around and call out the words "good luck" into the still, summer air. They may not have heard that back in Pennsylvania, but I'm sure they feel what we are all wishing their way—luck, but especially thanks and appreciation for representing Huntington Beach in such stellar fashion.

Our own little remarkable Boys of Summer, whose feats back east I hope many will always treasure right here at Murdy Park, now our own little hallowed baseball landmark.

Congratulations to all the fine teams back east—and a special thank-you, Ocean View Little League, for demonstrating such a high standard of graceful excellence.

Chapter 6

BUSINESSES

ALICE'S RESTAURANT (PART 1)

A little boy blows out a blue candle that's sticking out of a freshly baked cinnamon bun. The parents didn't ask for that, but when the server heard it was the boy's very first birthday, well, she just thought that was the proper thing to do. At a large table in the middle of the room, a group of girlfriends who look like they've know each other fifty or more years are having a raucous time, a dozen conversations overlapping at once.

Mary Beth Gustafson, "Baker Extraordinaire," as her card says, is in the kitchen with her twenty-one-year-old daughter, Kerstin, baking more of her legendary, mouth-watering cinnamon rolls from scratch, just like they've always been made. It seems pretty much everything at Alice's Breakfast in the Park restaurant is made in a way that would cause any old-fashioned Grandma to rejoice—made from scratch and with love.

Inside the small dining room, famously cluttered with charming bits of Americana, Alice Gustafson, seventy-seven, shares a table with me and her friend of some thirty-six years, Mary Kay McCauley. Amid the dolls, birdcages, fans, framed paintings, strung plastic lights and more, she's fretting a bit over a cup of strong coffee. As you may have heard, the Alice's in the Park era is now like a sun setting on the horizon here at the quiet end of the park by the lake. She told me her rent is being doubled and the city has bigger designs for the magical little place she's run since the early 1980s. Ironically, it was the city back then that asked Alice and husband,

The exterior of Alice's in the Park not long before the restaurant was shuttered.

John, based on their successful End Café at the edge of the pier, to actually open an establishment in the park. "Back when they did business with a handshake," Alice says. "When your word was law," adds Mary Kay. But today, things have changed.

The city has stated that it finds the property "underutilized" and would prefer to have a "café/bistro" in the park where alcohol could be served to up the checks. As Dana Parsons recounted recently in the *Los Angeles Times*, Alice "pays 'rent' to the city as part of a sliding tax on her sales. The increase the city wants, she says, would double her monthly payment." And she just can't afford that. Our breakfast comes a moment later, and it's as good as always. Freshly baked bread, perfect eggs and perhaps the best sausage I'll ever eat.

How things reached this nadir varies somewhat depending on which side you're talking to. Alice's son, John, told me that if you broke it down, his mom works for about ten cents an hour. But that's okay because he says it never was about the money—it's just been about the people. He also says they did what they were supposed to in their deal with the city, and at this point he thinks the city just wants the site to generate more money. "I wish she could simply run the restaurant to the public's benefit until Labor Day 2010," he says. "Then she could retire and let the place go. That's all she wants." But the Huntington Beach director of economic development, Stanley Smalewitz, told me that too much additional deterioration would be incurred in that time. (Alice says she's kept up with whatever the city has asked for until now.) Plus, proposals for the "bistro" are already being reviewed by the city, so it's too late. "Bistro?" Mary Kay asks in disgust. "In this neighborhood? Drinking at a nighttime establishment in Central Park…bistro?"

At the counter, a petition to save Alice's started by a customer, Richard Reinbolt, boasts hundreds of signatures, with more being added each hour. For years he and his friend Guila let their pooch, Amber, chase ducks by Alice's (Amber passed away in August). He told me he started the petition because of how much he loves not just the place but what the place stands for. Part of the petition reads, "Alice's restaurant is a warm, wholesome, 28-year-old INSTITUTION, beloved and patronized by a large number of families and children from many locales for many years. Such an institution, characterized by its charming lakefront and quacking and honking residents needs to be regarded as SACRED to City Values and, therefore, free from being victimized by City Revenue Exploitation and promise of a glossy Bistro restaurant."

I am not really objective about this. I believe that cities are made more valuable by places like Alice's (I have out-of-town relatives who want to go there first thing when they visit). Places where children grow up, where old friends catch up and where time slows down to a nice peaceful pace have all but been vanquished from this city and many others. This represents a loss of more than just restaurant—it's the death of another bit of decency, uniqueness and community. Money runs a city, yes. But I believe some things have a value that transcends mere dollars and cents. Some places, like Alice's, are strong threads in a community's fabric, and measuring their value in strict financial terms seems shortsighted. There are bigger things at stake.

Will the neighborhood welcome a public park "bistro" that stays open late, builds traffic and serves booze? I don't know. Will the city make a lot more money on the site once it is done being "underutilized"? I don't care. Will people miss Alice's and feel like they've lost a part of their family once it's gone? I don't doubt it. Not for one second.

ALICE'S RESTAURANT (PART II)

"There will come a time when you believe everything is finished. That will be the beginning." So wrote Louis L'Amour, and had "America's

Storyteller" ever tasted one of the cinnamon rolls at Alice's in the Park, he might have asked afterward, "Uhm, and where might these be sold after everything is finished?"

That's one of several questions that arose naturally last Sunday morning as proprietor Alice Gustafson and I had breakfast one last time in her restaurant.

One last time because last Sunday was her last day in business.

And so, for a lazy couple of hours, Alice, my son Charlie and our friend Richard Reinbolt sat and talked, laughed and dabbed a few tears.

It was important to me that Richard join us for a couple of reasons. First, it was two years ago that he and I met because of Alice's. I'd written a couple columns in this paper decrying the fact that the city seemed bent on evicting Alice over lease issues. Richard (a regular customer) went further, gathering two thousand signatures on a petition, and, in a memorable speech, made his case at a city council meeting (along with Alice and many others). Their efforts bought the place two years so Alice could go out the way she intended—on her own terms.

The former schoolteacher totally won me over with his tenacious, erudite command of the situation. We became friends.

Second, Richard also suffered a tragic loss recently. The woman he adored died of cancer, and we had a long-promised plan to meet at Alice's and talk about his beloved Guila. Alice's is a place where you'd do important things like celebrate birthdays and anniversaries and recall memories of a loved one.

And so on this last day, we looked at photos of Guila and talked about her.

Of course, we talked about Alice too. Weary but still twinkle-eyed, the woman who for more than twenty years ran this little treasure of a place smiled gamely. "This place was never about the money, just the people," she told us. In between our meal, longtime customers came over to pay their respects. "This is the last breakfast, not the Last Supper," Richard said to lighten the mood.

The world-famous cinnamon rolls arrived. Perfect as always. Many of the knickknacks had come down, but the place still had a cozy, parlor-meets-attic atmosphere, like we'd tumbled into some nostalgic little rabbit hole where civility, manners and good conversation still count for something.

We talked about other local institutions that faded to black, like the Golden Bear, the Surf Theater, the Standard Market and the End Café (which was run by Alice's late husband, John). Everyone seems to wish those places were still here, as people undoubtedly will when they recall Alice's.

Alice, *right*, is seen here posing with her daughter Mary Beth, *left*, and her granddaughter Kerstin, *center*.

Will there ever be a marker here in the park that identifies this little corner where so many found joy and comfort? I hope so.

We talk about whether the new owner will tear down or preserve the structure. Hard to say. (Alice doesn't know who the new owner might be.)

We talk about what will happen to the dozens of ducks and geese that come around for feed. In time, when they realize the food source is gone, they'll probably just move on.

I asked Alice if there was anything she wanted to let her guests know after all these years. She started to speak, but then her eyes welled up, and she smiled and shrugged her shoulders. A moment later, she simply said, "Just thank you."

At the front door, we examined, one last time, the map Alice posted years ago for guests to mark with a pushpin where they came from. The map of the world is covered. We locals loved it, but it's hard to even gauge the number of foreigners whose image of Huntington Beach was positively shaped by Alice's.

As I was finishing this column, my friend the singer Franki Doll, whom I wrote about here recently, dropped me this note: "Not many people know this, but this building was opened at night where there were AA meetings held there for years, it was a home to many friends who found not only great food during the morning, but sobriety and hope at night after business hours. That little building changed lives."

That little building changed lives. How wonderfully put.

So you know, Mary Beth (Alice's daughter) will continue baking, and you can still order those luscious cinnamon rolls and follow her future at marybethsbakery.com.

Alice will get some much-needed rest and no doubt will think about her restaurant every day.

As for the rest of us, I guess we'll just have to savor our memories of a little place by a lake where kids fed the ducks and where friends and family slowed down a little to enjoy made-from-scratch meals prepared with love. A safe, inviting sanctuary that felt like home—at least the home we keep in our hearts.

"A little building that changed lives."

As I prepared this column, an idea for a poem came to mind, so I wrote it down. At the risk of exposing how much of a poet I am not, I'd still like to offer it here, as it seems to have been inspired by the closing of Alice's.

"Alice's"
The sun it sets
along the line
that measures life
my own and thine

can celebrate
what just has been
a lovely day
and in the wind

we bid farewell
to youthful dreams
old promises
pull at the seams

of fragile hearts
that race at night

until the dawn
when rosy light

resets the line
with calm and grace
new fields to roam
new dreams to chase

ICE, ICE BABY

It is well below freezing, and I'm starting to shiver. Ice is piled over my head, and my breath is coming out in thick, cold puffs. Just an average day in Huntington Beach, right? It is if you're standing in the freezer at Brewster's Ice on Sixth Street, just off Main, where I had the pleasure of visiting one recent balmy morning.

Fourth of July is one of the busiest times of the year here at one of the oldest businesses in town (it's actually the oldest owned by the original proprietors),

The venerable Brewster's Icehouse, which has been keeping things cold since 1945.

but Mike Costello still took some time to talk to me in between hauling blocks of ice off a delivery truck. He's worked here for twenty-two years, and he's married to Ellen Brewster, whose dad started this cool operation back in 1945. In this high-tech, gadget-obsessed era, Brewster's Ice may be the most refreshingly low-tech spot in California. The funky old blue and white rectangular building that houses it began life as an army-issue meat locker down on the beach during World War II (it stored the food that was used to feed soldiers at the gun encampments). After the Brewsters took it over in the mid-'40s, the building was moved to its current location, and today, it holds a small office, lots of ice and that's about it.

Mike explains that twice a week, the ice truck arrives with big blocks of freshly cut ice, but for Fourth of July week, it might be twice that. Over the years, Brewster's Ice has evolved through the eras as best it can, and Mike's fully aware that many young people today are oblivious to the fact that years ago, an "ice man" would deliver blocks of the frozen stuff to both families and businesses. That would have been Virgil Brewster, who carved a reputation for himself as one of the hardest-working local merchants the city has ever known. He'd lug one-hundred-pound blocks of ice on his back all through town, looking at the cardboard hexagonal measuring signs folks would post in their windows. The arrows might point at twenty, fifty or one hundred pounds, which determined how much ice they'd want that day. He'd lug ice over to the old Golden Bear, the Surf Theater and most restaurants—if you wanted ice you'd call Brewster's, plain and simple. Virgil passed away twelve or so years ago, but his wife, Lucille, still lives in town. She's ninety-seven years old, and if you come by Brewster's late Tuesday and Thursday mornings and Mike's not there, it's with good reason: that's when he takes Lucille bowling (and she can still break one hundred).

As I chat with Mike, Alice Gustafson arrives for her ice. Alice runs the wonderful Alice's in the Park, and her presence adds an interesting layer of history to Brewster's Ice—you realize how entwined some of our city's most reliable, precious businesses are with one another. A visit to Brewster's Ice also provides a peek at the history of Huntington Beach. You see, back when Virgil and Lucille ran the place, they'd also spend time in a cozy 1920s bungalow hidden among the thick trees just behind the icehouse. The charming cottage is still tucked back there, and Mike sometimes spends time inside, chilling out when things get quiet.

As for the product, you might think you know ice, but until you hear it explained, believe me—you don't know ice. I learn about all the basic grinds: "fine crushed," which is good for ice cream, *almost* good

Mike Costello, who married into the Brewster family and has run the icehouse for more than twenty years.

for Sno-Cones and just what you want for margaritas. Then there's the "business crush" grind, still used by a few businesses for fountain drinks. "Heavy crush" grind is used for cooling in ice chests, and last but not least, the "party ice" grind is your basic cubed ice for parties (which used to be mechanically sawed until the machinery became too expensive—now the ice is put into tumblers to cube it).

There's dry ice as well (most popular at Halloween). Did you know that if you put dry ice in a chest topped with three inches of crushed on top, it makes a "refrigerator" that will last for eight to ten days?

You must also know that not all ice is created equal. Mike tells me that white ice is not good—it means that there's too much air in the ice, and thus, it will melt faster. You want to always look for clear ice, which is all you'll ever find at Brewster's.

Brewster's Ice is one of those places that's a snapshot of the past, recalling days of simpler industry, a time when streetcar conductors, door-to-door salesmen and, yes, ice men were all part of neighborhoods. Virgil Brewster may be gone, but thankfully, his family is still moving blocks of ice here in Huntington Beach (and, even better, his missus is still bowling).

Let's raise a nice cold glass to Brewster's Ice.

LOCAL LEGEND

The big, yellowed 1940s clock hanging on the garage wall works like it always has. Under the clock's thick glass, the second hand moves fluidly, never stopping, smooth and steady. It's a classic. "Just like she ran in the dealership," laughs Bob Terry.

For years in Huntington Beach, Bob's family ran one of the best-known businesses in city history, the venerable Terry Buick just off Pacific Coast Highway on Fifth Street (across from another local institution, the Surf Theater). The old clock and Bob are just about all that remains from the dealership—that is, except for Bob's lovely wife, Dolores, who also worked at Terry Buick.

We're talking in the Terrys' well-kept home, just a baseball toss from Huntington Beach High School, where Bob played in the 1950s. More on that in a bit.

Bob represented Huntington Beach at Governor Pat Brown's Conference on Youth. He was Citizen of the Year here in 1981, founded

Bob Terry, whose family ran one of the most popular automobile showrooms in Huntington Beach.

the Downtown Merchants Guild, created the first-ever street fair in 1981—and the list goes on.

Bob was born in 1937, the year his dad, Collins "Pop" Terry, opened his new showroom (he started as a Pontiac dealer in 1926). Covering the Terrys' living room table are dozens of photos, letters, business cards and scrapbooks. The family started here in 1909 (an aunt was the first to arrive), and the Terrys clearly made a lasting impact. Relatives eventually owned many buildings and businesses in town, so much so that the area near the car dealership and family gas station was dubbed "Terryville" in the 1960s.

Bob's childhood memories of Huntington Beach are not exactly idyllic. "I was miserable," he laughs. "I had asthma, and in October, when they'd thrash the lima bean fields—you have to remember those were a huge crop here—my asthma and allergies made me feel awful. I'd be in bed for weeks at a time."

At eight years old, the only child started working at the dealership, riding his bike from his house at the corner of Eleventh and Main Streets. "I'd sweep, do whatever my dad needed, after school. I'd pump gas and shine the teeth on those classic Buick grills. After school, Saturday, all the time through college. My father decided when I was one year old that I'd run the family business someday," Bob says wistfully. "He liked being a mechanic, but he didn't like running the business part, so that became my destiny."

How did that sit with Bob? Not well. "In the summer of '57, my American Legion baseball coach got me a tryout with the Milwaukee Braves. I was a six foot five pitcher, lefty, and I could throw hard, so they offered me a contract to go with the team and have a coach work with me. I took the contract home. My dad tore it up and said, 'Baseball players are nothing but bums—you're working for me.' And I'm still mad at him today."

After graduating from USC in 1960, Bob was put right to work full time—put in charge, in fact—and discovered he had a knack for selling cars. Seven years later, "Pop" passed away, leaving Bob as the youngest Buick dealer in the nation. "But all I wanted to do was play baseball," Bob says, shaking his head slowly.

Nevertheless, the business thrived, and Bob became a fixture in Huntington Beach until the mid-1980s. It was then, during the overhaul of downtown, that the dealership was lost. Bitterness remains between Bob and city officials over how things were handled.

"Too much to go into," he says. "That's why I've been invisible for a lot of years. I co-founded Huntington Savings after the whole dealership debacle with downtown, and today I work for a mortgage company in Santa

Ana. But now, with the centennial and all, I'm more in the mood to talk about my family's history in Huntington Beach. It's been very amicable with the chamber of commerce, of which I used to be on the board, and today I've just been thinking that there should maybe be a plaque near where the dealership used to be. That's what's got me talking again—not just my family history, but there's other places, so many places knocked down, and don't you think people would like to learn about those stories? I really think it would be a good way to go."

That is what has Bob breaking his silence—the simple yearning to have his family's important history documented in town. I cannot agree more. Bob's pictures alone tell a story of a family that made huge contributions to Huntington Beach. I've written about this before, but what better time than now to create a marker program in town to acknowledge this and other relevant family histories in town?

Terry Buick sponsored countless charities here, from the Boys Club to Little League. I think it'd be good for the city to give something back to Bob and his family's remarkable Huntington Beach legacy.

Meanwhile, as sure as the old Terry clock will keep time, Bob will keep organizing his photos and family history—and watching for baseballs that manage to make it over from the high school and into his yard.

Meet Mr. Meat

"I don't know how many tons," he says pensively, this big, solid man dressed all in black, with jet-black hair and a silver, longhorn-shaped bolo tie. "Near six tons—and that's just prime rib."

Six tons. Just prime rib. And he's describing just what he'll sell during the holiday season.

The man is Calvin Free, and the place is the Beef Palace. This meat-worshiper's Mecca has been in Huntington Beach for forty years now, opened by Free's dad, the legendary butcher Melvin Free.

"He told me he was the greatest butcher who ever lived, and he may have been right," Free chuckles as he moves around his so-spotless-you-could-eat-off-the-floor shop like a kid in a candy store, only instead of candy, it's top-grade steaks, hams, sausages, pork chops, ribs, lamb chops, tri-tips, filets, sushi-grade fish—and the prime rib that's become the stuff of legend.

"We sell more prime rib at this time of year than any place in Southern California—maybe even the whole state," Free says, examining a row of giant hindquarters that are hanging in full view behind the counter.

"This is part of the dry-aging process," he says proudly, examining the racks the way Rocky did before pounding them. "We like customers to see part of how we do it, this four- to five-week process that makes what we consider to be the most tender, flavorful prime rib you'll ever taste."

Photos along the wall tell the story: dozens of customers lined up over the years as they wait for the gold—one of the Beef Palace's prized, dry-aged prime ribs.

Of course, there's more to the Beef Palace than just splendid prime rib. This is a shop that's become a part of people's lives over the years.

"I think it's because my dad was an old-school butcher who, by the time he opened this shop, was well known as a butcher. It was his life," Free says, standing near a pyramid of marinades and barbecue sauces. "He understood that a community needed a neighborhood butcher that had the highest standards."

The freethinking Calvin Free runs the Beef Palace, in the author's opinion the best place for meat in the city.

Melvin Free, who started with his brothers in San Diego, died in the 1990s, but his son thinks of him often. "I hear him in my head all the time," he beams. "He set the standard, and I just follow it."

Free works himself to the bone (so to speak) to buy the best for his customers—many of whom have become more like fans than just mere clientele.

The grinding mill Free's dad put out front so that customers could watch their fresh meat become bright red hamburger is still there, still used. But perhaps the most old-fashioned touch is Free himself, a boisterous, positive man who loves what he does and is not afraid to advertise it.

"Christmas is the time when we remind ourselves what it is we do," he grins. "It's our time to be at our best for folks."

But Free makes sure the Beef Palace shines all year. He recounts several years ago, when the city asked if he'd donate some hamburgers for a Fourth of July barbecue for the marines at the Newland House. "Hamburger?" Free laughs. "Not for the marines. I said, 'They eat rib eyes, and I'm cooking them.'"

Since then, the city has adopted the Third Battalion, First Marine Regiment, First Marine Division at Camp Pendleton, and often, Free keeps them fed—with steaks.

As I talk with Free behind the busy counter, Kathleen Regan walks in to pick up the gift certificate that Free donates to the Village View Elementary School's Grandparents' Day basket. On the spot, Free doubles the amount.

"I've lived here thirty-two years," Regan tells me. "As a little girl, we'd come in here and they'd give me a hot dog or some bologna while my mom shopped. Today, they do that for my two children, who are ten and eight. And, of course, my kids ride the cows."

She speaks, of course, of the two giant ceramic cows at the front of the store—recognizable landmarks to anyone who has visited the shop.

Free knows he has a responsibility to customers like Regan and others. "After 9/11, I had little old ladies come in here, lifelong customers, asking me if I could sharpen their knives in case they needed to protect themselves. We're connected to this community in ways I'm not sure I'll ever understand," Free shrugs. "But I love it."

Now, if you're reading this column on the Thursday when the *Independent* comes out, I will tell you that you have just one day to order what may just be the world's best prime rib from what is certainly one of the world's best butcher shops and have it in time for Christmas. The demand is just that great. You've been warned—order *now*.

A seasoned ten-pounder will be on the Epting table this Christmas.

Behind me, Free is laughing and kibitzing with customers like they're family. And in a way they are. This is a man who loves what he does—in a place that both he and the community love. What a nice fit.

Fireworks

"I like the big ones," he giggled with an almost sinister glee.

Clearly this guy loves his job.

"The eight-inch shells are great, but that time during the '84 Olympics when we got to launch two twenty-four-inch shells—140 pounds each—man! It took two people to load them into a mortar buried thirteen feet into the ground and 15 pounds of black powder to blast them two thousand feet in the air!"

Meet Jeff Eidemiller, chief pyrotechnician for the Zambelli Fireworks Internationale Company. He's also the man in charge of your Huntington Beach fireworks spectacular this Fourth of July.

I'm speaking to him while he's in Stockton, producing a fireworks show for a couple's fiftieth wedding anniversary. In terms of spectacle, Jeff says it's the same size show Surf City will be getting. One can only imagine the light in the wife's eyes as the couple celebrates their golden moment together.

Jeff, who's downright giddy when talking fireworks, tells me that our show will include some 1,500 rounds—making it the largest attended fireworks display west of the Rockies.

He's been "shooting" (his term) for the legendary Zambellis since 1981, and it's hard to imagine a better man for the job. His energy and enthusiasm crackle like so many summer sparklers, and it's evident that our local show is in the right hands. (Zambelli, so you know, is proudly known as the "First Family of Fireworks," and it is one of the oldest and largest American fireworks companies.)

Jeff's responsibilities for producing shows such as this entail everything—setting up the equipment, managing the crew, loading the fireworks, making sure the display is fired according to plan and even the post-show cleanup. He crafts the musical soundtrack as well, and this year the theme is "Let Freedom Ring," featuring patriotic music from Ray Charles, Toby Keith and the Philadelphia Philharmonic, among other artists.

The fifty-four-year-old shooter started in the business at age seventeen in Arcadia, where he grew up. His pyro skills have taken him around the world,

Fireworks have long been part of the tradition here in Huntington Beach.

creating shows in Australia, Mexico, Canada and many other places. He's worked at Disneyland, all Six Flags parks, the *Queen Mary*, concerts by the Who and Garth Brooks and many other events.

His favorite gig thus far? The seven years he spent each July atop Mount Rushmore, blasting airborne, candy-colored explosives into the black night above the Black Hills of South Dakota.

Today, he produces about eighteen shows a year. His favorite specific firework is a specialty shell that produces a happy face in midair. He explains that the design is created by the burst charge in the middle of the shell, which looks just like a happy face and is simply expanded once the shell explodes.

Interestingly, this is simply a hobby for the gleeful shooter. Eidemiller works for the California Water Service Company up near Los Gatos as senior technician in charge of the computer pump controls. But his weekends are made for fireworks shows.

A purist at heart, he designs his productions using electricity instead of computers, thus allowing for the human element of actually pushing a button that launches the blasts. "Hand fired is better," he says. "You feel it. And when you hear the crowd react, well, that's why we do it."

Our spectacular this year marks something special for Eidemiller too. His daughter, twenty-three-year-old Caty, will be firing the show along with her dad. She's next in the family line, and if she's anything like Jeff, she's sure to have a blast.

Chapter 7

In Memoriam

The Coach (Part I)

Wednesday of last week was such a strange day. The mercury pushed up near one hundred degrees throughout the region, the sort of strange, unseasonably arid kind of day that will prompt at least a few to start wondering about "earthquake weather." It was a summer day that didn't happen all summer, and the odd, almost-eerie stillness that comes with such an afternoon was obliterated at about 1:30 p.m. when a gunman in Seal Beach opened fire, killing eight innocent people (and injuring a ninth).

The sickening, hollow feeling we get on the heels of such news is profound. Little did I know that that same evening (with temperatures still a balmy ninety), I'd witness something so beautiful that it, at least for several moments, would actually eclipse the brutal events in Seal Beach and cast a glow (literally) that saved the day.

Coach Jim Harris, sixty-seven, at Ocean View High School is a local legend. I know his name, accomplishments and reputation cast a longer shadow than just Huntington Beach, but for the locals, he is a legend.

He has coached at Ocean View for thirty-three years, since the school opened. Teams he has led have won nineteen basketball league championships on the boys' side, and several years ago, he even had a five-season stint coaching Ocean View's girls' basketball team, which won four league titles during that time.

Talk to alumni, though, and it's not the numbers that his legend is built around—it's the man. Harris's leadership skills combined with his compassion and concern for students have resulted in a remarkable small-town love affair between players, students, parents—and coach.

Recently, my friend Lanna Briggs Miller, a member of the first-ever graduating class of OVHS (and as sparklingly enthusiastic an alumni as can be found), made me aware that Coach had recently been diagnosed with cancer and was having a very rough time. Almost immediately, Facebook groups popped up so former and current students and families could begin posting messages of support for Coach Harris.

Pages and pages of heartfelt missives appeared each day. Not knowing Coach personally, I began to get a sense of a great man who has touched countless lives for the better. The image of a vital father figure emerged from men, women and children alike.

Lanna also told me that last Wednesday, a candlelight vigil, organized by Tracy King-Wenschlag, would take place outside the Harris residence in Fountain Valley. King-Wenschlag, whose five children either graduated from OVHS or attend there now, had been inspired by Harris years earlier after her husband died and the coach stepped in to help make sure her sons had a positive role model.

Before the vigil, attendees were made aware that the coach would probably be unable to come outside, but he would be home, and fully aware, that many from his past would be outside united in prayer, faith and love.

I arrived at the cul-de-sac where the coach lives just before 7:00 p.m. amidst dozens of others who were approaching the house. The mood as people approached the house was wistful and reflective—not unlike a high school reunion. One woman remembered babysitting on the street where the Harris family lives. Another recalled a 1980s party that took place nearby.

Small children, teenagers and adults moved en masse toward the end of the street, the crowd swelling to more than 150 people. But as they reached the house, the mood settled. Candles were lit, thoughts were gathered and people shared shouts of encouragement to the coach and his family, who were visible just inside a front window. The orange-yellow candle flames glowed and danced in what felt like a tropical breeze.

They didn't expect to see the coach; that wasn't the point. As King-Wenschlag told me, her vision for the event was simply to let the coach see them—to let him know how much they cared.

But then, unexpectedly, the door opened. And out came Coach, assisted by Kim and Shane Morris, his daughter and son-in-law.

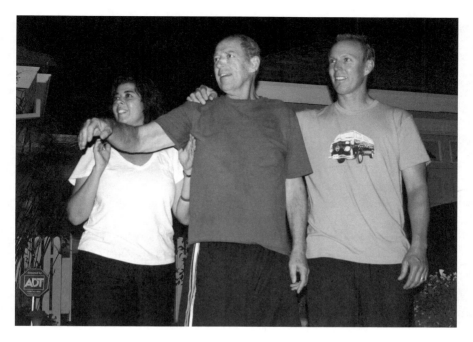

Coach Jim Harris from Ocean View High School the night he came out to greet all those who came to pay him tribute at his house—one of the most moving nights of this author's life.

People started to cheer at first, a natural reaction, but they caught themselves so as not to overwhelm Coach (or the moment).

In a strong voice, he thanked everyone. He hugged Lanna. Then he added, "Well, you saved me once before."

Harris was referring to an incident in 1985. As the *Los Angeles Times* reported March 29 of that year, "Nearly one-quarter of the students at Ocean View High School in Huntington Beach walked out of classes Thursday morning and staged a 30-minute sit-in outside Principal John Myers' office to protest his decision to relieve basketball coach Jim Harris of his duties." (Harris had been the target of a three-month investigation into athlete-recruitment practices.)

Students created petitions and protested even louder. Then this was the story in the *Times* on May 15, 1985: "Jim Harris, the Ocean View High School basketball coach who was relieved of his coaching duties less than two months ago, was reinstated to his position as head coach Tuesday. Several of Harris' players and other students circulated petitions at the school and in surrounding businesses Thursday calling for his reinstatement."

The kids helped save him then, and several who had protested back in '85 were there holding candles last Wednesday.

Annamarie Briones, class of 1987 (whose son Mark is class of 2013), told me, "We all walked out of class at the same time and sat down in the commons. We were all protesting. It was the only way people would listen to us about how much he meant to us. Not only is he a coach, he is a mentor, a teacher and all-around wonderful person who makes you want to be a better person."

After Coach turned and was helped back into his house, King-Wenschlag led the crowd in "Amazing Grace." Lanna led them in the school fight song. And then candles were silently hoisted once more, a glowing beacon of strength for the coach to see.

Afterward, I asked Tracy why it was so important for her to organize this event. "When my son Anthony's father died of cancer, it was very tough. Coach became a real role model—a positive influence. Today, my son's name is on the wall of fame in the gym. That's because of how Coach worked with him to get there as a varsity basketball player. All of my kids have been positively affected by him. Just like everyone else here tonight."

As the crowd started to disperse, the candles were extinguished, but the prayers and good thoughts no doubt will continue to burn bright for Coach Harris. Quietly, the students and former students walked away after having created a sublime moment of respect, honor and love on a day when many of us, especially the coach, needed it most.

Wednesday of last week was such a strange day.

But what I'll remember most will be the candles.

Our prayers are with you, Coach Harris.

And yes, clearly, your kids are ready to help save you again.

THE COACH (PART II)

The week before last, Coach Jim Harris from Ocean View High School addressed a candlelight vigil outside his home with grace, calm and characteristic fight. The aggressive cancer that had been diagnosed in August had clearly taken its toll, but in the warm night air, his spirit still soared. On the wings of the faithful students who had gathered, he seemed uplifted.

But then, just like that, he is gone.

Harris, who coached basketball for thirty-three years at Ocean View, who won nineteen league championships and three Southern Section titles, passed away Sunday night at the age of sixty-seven.

The beloved coach's legacy was secure long before he became ill, yet as the specter of the sickness became more insidious over the last few weeks, living, breathing shrines were born on Facebook. Students from days gone by poured their hearts out each day, eloquently capturing their vivid love and respect for Coach Harris. They were hoping and praying for the best but preparing for the worst.

Monday night, the doors of the Ocean View gym were open as usual. Like primal music, the sound of basketballs being dribbled punched a precise, rapid-fire melody in the night. That's the pulse of the Harris legacy, that beautiful sound of ball-on-court, punctuated by whistles, Coach's commands and the squeak of fresh sneakers on hardwood. This is Hoosiers-by-the-sea for many who have gone here, a big noisy gym built up from nothing but hard work, commitment and discipline.

And a coach.

Outside, a small shrine of candles and photos had been arranged by the front door. Lana Briggs-Miller, class of '80, who helped organize the candlelight vigil, was dutifully arranging things in preparation for a last-minute, informal memorial gathering in the gym—still an effervescent cheerleader for her school, her coach and the memory that must now be served.

Dozens of people began to arrive, many eyes moist with tears. Long, silent hugs were exchanged. Then, as they'd all done so many times before, they filed into the gym. Not for a game but to form a circle around center court, where a lone basketball sat.

Bob Briggs, Lana's brother, took out his trumpet and powerfully pierced the silence with the spiritual hymn "Goin' Home" followed by the school Alma Mater.

Cody Whitewold, class of '80, guided the group with a series of prayerful offerings. Then, holding hands, the group of several dozen went around the circle sharing stories, laughs and tears, united in their love of a fallen leader.

Outside, some younger students stood silently near the vigil, paying tribute. One, Elvi Delgado, class of '09, was particularly upset. She wrote a long message on a tall glass candle with a black Sharpie pen, carefully choosing her words as her lip quivered. When she was done composing her message to the coach, she talked about him, revealing what I think may be the most impressive quality in a man who had many.

Elvi Delgado pays tribute to Coach Harris outside the Ocean View Gym at the memorial held just after the coach passed away.

Delgado spoke not so much about Harris the coach but Harris the teacher. And father figure. She told me how she currently works two jobs. She sends money home to Mexico to help support her recently deported father. And more. She is a very young woman dealing with very adult responsibilities, and her ability to do so, she says, came in large part from Harris. "He always told me that hard work will make a positive difference in my life, that I can do anything I want to if I try hard enough and to believe in myself. He took time to make me feel like I belonged, and he looked out for me and gave me guidance. He helped me grow up and understand the importance of taking responsibility. He was just the most wonderful teacher."

The cardinal and gold banners will wave long and proud for Coach Harris. Things will be named in his honor because of what he accomplished with his players. As they should be. But as big an impact as he made on the court and in the locker rooms, guiding his players, let it not be forgotten that he also played a vital role in many other students' lives. This was a teacher first, after all, who extended himself not just to towering centers and playmaking point guards but to everyone who needed him.

Elvi Delgado left quietly, and soon the gym emptied as well. People said their goodbyes and headed off into the parking lot, leaving behind the soft glow of candlelight and the sound of those basketballs, still echoing in the night.

Every community has a giant or two, those who tower over the rest of us, cast longer shadows and command respect thanks to their sheer gravity. They leave bigger footprints, and the echoes of their voices seem to linger longer than others.

That was Coach Jim Harris, as evidenced by the love that's being expressed now and certainly for generations to come. To the Harris family, we send our deepest condolences and prayers as they deal with their loss.

But collectively, I know a community also says thank you to the family for sharing someone who understood how important it was to make a positive difference.

Someone who cared.

A winner. A teacher.

A giant.

THE REV

I'm sitting here trying to make sense of and write this column about what I witnessed last week: the two services I attended for Jimmy "The Rev" Sullivan, drummer (who wrote and sang) for the Huntington Beach–based band Avenged Sevenfold.

This tightknit family knew early that the little boy banging on toys in the tub was destined for something percussive—but as the member of a spectacularly popular band?

"The Rev" tragically passed away at twenty-eight the week before last, and while nobody is quite sure what happened, it really doesn't matter. What's important is that a family here misses their son (and brother).

Joe and Barbara Sullivan want to address the fans soon, and they will. For now, not as a columnist but as a friend, I asked their permission to convey the power of what I witnessed at the services, and they said it was OK. But as I sit here, it's hard to know where to begin.

This lovely family (including Jimmy's sisters Kelly and Katie) was visible at the services not just gracefully tending to the assembled flock but also on the several scrapbook photo boards at the church featuring hundreds of family photos. Vacations, camping trips, birthdays, ballgames, Jimmy

The Sullivan family in 2001.

playing one of his first sets of drums—they all grew up right before our eyes.

So how do you begin to write of the vastness of this loss the family is feeling? I can tell you that as friends and family paid tribute to The Rev at the rosary service the night before the funeral, it was powerful, heartfelt and real—just like The Rev himself. The packed church was treated to stories from pals, relatives and his first drum teacher, who spoke of the young boy who understood and executed polyrhythmic theory in a matter of weeks.

Grade-school buddies recalled the happy-go-lucky athlete who became a real-life rock star but never forgot where he came from. The four remaining members of Avenged Sevenfold entered together and then rose together to address the crowd. Tearfully, these young men, wives and girlfriends by their sides, shared their love of their band mate.

Finally, The Rev's dad, Joe Sullivan, spoke about his son, honoring him with an eloquent speech on how much he learned from his boy—and how it will affect his life going forward. There was pain in the room, but it was trumped by joy and love generated by The Rev, whom many felt comfortable, justifiably, in calling their best friend.

The funeral the next day was an equally dramatic, beautiful event. In addition to the hundreds of family and friends gathered (including Jimmy's fiancée, Leana), there were several bands in attendance, including members of Buckcherry and My Chemical Romance. Flowers, cymbals and drum heads signed by legendary bands were delivered, representing the love and respect among the bands' brethren.

Avenged Sevenfold guitarist Brian Haner, aka Synyster Gates, delivered a soaring eulogy with focus and class. You look at him and the other young men in the band—M. Shadows, Zacky Vengeance and Johnny Christ—and wonder what they must be feeling, but in their eyes, you see the pain of their loss.

I will tell you here that besides their music, what I love about Avenged Sevenfold is that they choose to remain part of Huntington Beach. They could easily have left after hitting it big, but they didn't. They bought homes here, they're known around town, they hire their buddies as crew; they're good guys. Rock stars? Whatever. They're hardworking, successful young men who got where they are because they're very good at what they do, and the city is better for having them here.

Back to the Sullivan family. As they clung together at the church and at the cemetery, surrounded by hundreds of mourners, it reminded one that the son they gave the world affected many lives—young lives. As I struggled trying to write this column, an e-mail arrived. It was from a young woman in Omaha, Nebraska, Rachel Lee. She's a twenty-two-year-old librarian who loves Avenged Sevenfold.

Sullivan Thanksgiving gathering. Jimmy can be seen at the left with glasses.

Her note read in part, "I specifically wanted to thank you for humanizing the drummer and his family, giving a sense of what those of us who have looked up at their stage and sung their lyrics, begged for their autographs, have only sensed at a distance—that at the end of the night their loved ones back in Huntington Beach are truly their family and their home.

"While the fandom has suffered a great loss, we dearly wish to express that they are not alone in their grief and there are a lot of us out there who wish we could do something to ease the pain of Jimmy's passing. Tonight, a candlelight vigil is being planned in a number of cities in his memory, fans gathering together to talk and laugh and remember The Rev."

She went on to tell me about a scrapbook project in honor of Jimmy being headed by a young woman in Florida, Victoria Deroy, who also wrote to express her sorrow over Jimmy's loss and her plan to help keep his memory alive. "Avenged Sevenfold saved my life, and from the moment I heard of Jimmy's death, I felt as though my entire world had fallen apart," Victoria wrote. "I wanted to comfort the men that I had grown to know and love through their music, DVDs and live performances. I sent out over 20 messages to fan pages and tried to get several of my friends involved and the end result was over 190 messages from fans all over the world. We received prayers, notes and stories, even from people who had known Jimmy personally. I am currently in the process of hand-crafting the scrapbook and will send it out as soon as I am finished."

Losses like this will never be easy for me to process, make sense of and write about, but the words of these fans brought some clarity. Jimmy's loss is being felt by millions all around the world—especially by a family and a band of brothers here in Huntington Beach.

If you haven't listened to Avenged Sevenfold, I recommend you do. It's raw, passionate music played with skill, soul and unbridled fury. My sixteen-year-old son, Charlie, adores this band, so we have had the benefit of hearing them constantly. As I write this, their song "Critical Acclaim" plays loudly, and proudly, behind me.

Listen to the music, listen to the magic and, by all means, listen to the backbeat thunder. There's no way better way to honor the Sullivan family—after all, that's their boy on the drums.

A SON SHINES

"It was sixteen weeks ago today," Chris Hernandez says quietly. He's referring to the horrific day of his son Christopher's accident. However, sitting with Chris and his wife, Dawn, the discussion is not sad. Naturally, it's tinged with sorrow given the weight of the tragedy, but four months on, both parents focus more on the peace they feel, made possible by their rock-solid faith in God. They talk about how the memory and spirit of their son motivates his friends, and they talk about the lessons their late son continues to teach them as they celebrate his life.

They also talk about the pain of having the awful event misreported and reshaped into sickening tabloid fodder by both a local newspaper and a Los Angeles TV station. For the record, once and for all, from a full-page release issued by the Huntington Beach Police Department, "There is no evidence to suggest that the accident was a result of car surfing…The distraction of misinformation by several media sources has…exasperated the grief the family has had to endure."

Got it? Yes, it was a tragic accident involving bad judgment by numerous parties. But contrary to many "news" outlets, it was not "car surfing." The vulture-like nature of the media today, along with the insensitive, anonymous jackals who take glee from posting vicious posts on various newspaper-supported blogs, are ugly parts of this modern world—but you can always beat them with facts.

I won't dwell anymore on these parasites because it's a personal rant and not at all what the Hernandez family wants. Rather, they want to focus on the positive, on doing what's best for their family and Christopher's legacy.

There's also something else, though, and I must admit, I think what I'm about to share you may not ever forget—and it's also something you may feel compelled to share with others.

Here we go.

Dawn, a doting, dedicated "mom's mom," is describing for me a primary source of her strength these days. It's the signs she receives from her son—messages of strength that she feels in her soul are her son reaching out to her. Her husband describes the same profound experiences. They've already had many moments like this between the two of them. But they've also had experiences relayed to them by others about their son.

Michael, who asked that his last name be withheld, was a good friend of Christopher. The day of the accident, the buddies had their guitars out and

Christopher Hernandez giving a speech at St. Bonaventure School in Huntington Beach.

were playing together. They even videotaped their performance. Michael's dad, a Hernandez family friend, heard the music that day.

"It was beautiful," he said. "The boys were locked in a moment with the music, in that spiritual way that musicians experience when everything is right."

At the rosary service for Christopher several days later, Michael's dad was incredibly moved. "The deacon used very beautiful words in talking about Christopher," he said. "He talked of guardian angels and Christopher still being here, and it struck me, this talk of angels. That's not something that's 'front and center' in the Catholic Church, or at least it's not something I'm used to hearing a lot about, and I found it very interesting."

The day of the funeral service, he was on his computer, looking up information on buying tickets. When it came time to make his search, the Ticketmaster website required that he input a series of random words as a security measure, as many of you have probably experienced yourselves.

But now it's all but impossible for me to believe there's anything random about it. You see, the two words that Michael's dad was instructed to type, on the day Christopher was laid to rest, at a time when he was feeling the pain of loss, while also focusing on the mystery of angels—the two words read: "beloveds Christopher."

That's right: "beloveds Christopher."

He was so stunned that he created a screen capture so that the Hernandez family would be able to experience this magic of the moment.

Today, he still finds it hard to find the words to describe the moment. "Maybe because I heard him play that music with my son a few days before, there was a connection. And maybe because he knew the pain his parents were in, he was just reaching out to me so that I could let his parents know he was OK. But it was like seeing a glimpse of heaven. It was Christopher reaching out and saying to all of us, 'I'm here and I'm all right. Everything is OK.' This was a glimpse of heaven."

Of all the words that could have popped up in this process (many of which are usually either nonsensical or incongruous), it was "beloveds Christopher." Take a deep, long moment and consider that.

This happened four months ago, and since then, there have been more enlightening episodes the Hernandez family has become aware of. There is a lot more to the journey, and as I said, this column will pick up the story next week. After all, we're entering a season of faith, a word that defines the Hernandez family.

By the way, the tickets that Michael's dad was shopping for when he was asked to type in "beloveds Christopher"? They were for the Angels.

DANNY THE DINOSAUR

It's about 5:45 a.m. on a Saturday. It's still dark and there's a light fog shrouding Main Street, yet down along the south side of the pier, there's activity. Several teenagers, surfboards in tow, are parking their bikes and making their way quietly toward the ocean. Closer to shore, in a gray, pre-dawn light, it's possible to make out the outline of a small table that's been set up. On it, several bunches of flowers have been arranged. In the next few minutes, more people arrive.

Teenagers are joined by adults, most carrying surfboards, some rubbing sleep from their eyes. There's some light discussion, mostly masked by the sound of the surf. There are also plenty of hugs and weak smiles. Some stretch out their muscles, while others apply wax to their boards. Dawn starts

A cross marks the spot where Danny Oates lost his life.

creeping in, pale yellow light through a thick purple sky. Fresh donuts have arrived on the table, and a woman wearing a lime green T-shirt is setting up a dispenser with hot coffee. On the back of her shirt in black letters are the words "In memory of Danny 'The Dinosaur' Oates."

By now, about sixty or so people have gathered on the beach. They're here to remember and celebrate Danny, who was killed a year ago. Just like now, it was that time of the year when kids go to school to see what teacher they'll have. That's all Danny (who would be entering high school this year) was doing last August, riding his bike to school, when a speeding truck driven by Jeffrey Woods plowed into him, taking his life instantly. (Woods has pleaded not guilty to vehicular manslaughter and driving under the influence, both felonies, and is scheduled to appear in court again in October.)

Last week I received a note from Danny's mom, Kristi: "Some of our great friends are hosting a memorial paddle out for Danny on Saturday. Surfing tradition dictates that surfers gather and do a memorial paddle out close to the date that the person passed on to celebrate their life…I cannot even begin to tell you what this community has done for our family since Danny was killed. I have so many unspoken thank you's that I don't even know where I would begin. When I sit down to begin the process of thanking my friends and community it's overwhelming to the point of paralyzing. The genuine caring and support we have received exceed anything I have ever experienced or witnessed."

Case in point, the many family and friends here on the beach. By the time Kristi and Paul Oates arrive, everyone's ready to paddle out for the ceremony, but not before taking a moment to share with the grieving parents.

Tom Clarke, a friend of the Oates family, has a son, Dylan, who was friends with Danny since first grade. "We're here to memorialize Danny and to support the family," Tom says. "We did this a year ago, and it was amazing. It's so quiet when you get out beyond the waves. We form a circle and then go around, one by one, sharing thoughts and memories of Danny. It's pretty powerful. It's important because it's get-togethers like this that help keep a memory alive, which is the most important thing when you lose someone you love." A moment or two later, Tom heads toward the surf with about forty or so other people, including Danny's dad. Flowers are being carried out to sea as well. Kristi Oates, along with some friends, heads up to the pier to watch the ceremony from above.

The ocean this morning is calm, and soon, a circle of humanity is bobbing gently near the end of the pier, banding closer together until each person is an arm's length from the next. From the pier, you can hear the din of their voices but not exact words. From Ruby's diner, an old song plays with a bit of static, as if it's broadcasting from a 1940s radio. The tune is a World War II standard that provides an appropriate lyrical soundtrack:

> *I'll be seeing you*
> *In all the old familiar places*
> *That this heart of mine embraces*
> *All day through…*

Suddenly, near the circle, a sea lion comes into view. He seems to be watching the ceremony from about twenty yards away, curiously popping in and out of the water, as if looking for an invite. A teenage girl on the pier whispers to her friend, "It's like Danny knows they're there and he just wants to say hello."

On the radio, the song plays out:

> *I'll find you*
> *In the morning sun*

The paddle-out for Danny Oates as it looked from the Huntington Beach pier.

And when the night is new.
I'll be looking at the moon,
But I'll be seeing you.

If you ever wonder about the power of what a community can do when it bands together in support of healing and friendship, look no further than this cluster of people at dawn—up on the pier and out in the ocean, in a circle, with an inquisitive sea lion as their audience.

DANE

As Valen Williams takes a seat in the family living room, B.B. King's "The Thrill Is Gone" plays on the radio. The song is apt, perhaps, because we are talking about the loss of her son, Dane Williams.

The twenty-three-year-old was reported missing in late January while attending a trade show near the Gaslamp Quarter in San Diego. Several

Images of Dane Williams with his family.

days later, his body was found in an alley in a downtrodden neighborhood about seven miles from where he was last seen.

To try to describe the impact of this event on Valen; Dane's dad, Jim; or sister, Hayley (not to mention Dane's many friends and associates), is simply not possible; it is just beyond words.

I'd never met Dane or his family, but this case left me reeling. Though there are many horrific events these days involving young people, this one just seemed to combine all the most basic qualities and elements designed to break your heart. The young man who, by every account, was good-natured, hardworking, well raised and a positive force on virtually everyone he came in contact with. A solid, tightknit Huntington Beach family.

He was just probably trying to get back to his hotel room after a long day. But he didn't make it. Something happened to him. And then, hours later, someone saw fit to leave his body, wrapped in an old blanket, in some nondescript alley.

I started following this case, and day after day, a sickening feeling grew inside of me: a catastrophic crime was committed here.

A photo of young Dane with his father, Jim.

And although it is unsolved, it had all but dropped from view. Sure, there were the recent stories that highlighted his blood alcohol level. OK, he'd had a few drinks—but he wasn't driving and did not appear by anyone to be drunk. I think that's what drove me to call Valen. To clear up some of the misrepresentation and, more importantly, to refocus attention on this case. For about an hour last week, I listened to Valen explain, in controlled yet emotional sentences, the many frustrations she and her family are experiencing. The investigation in San Diego has yet to produce any concrete answers. I called San Diego Police lieutenant Kevin Rooney of the homicide unit to inquire about the case but have yet to hear back.

Valen describes the tortured hours soon after learning Dane was missing. The legal red tape needed to review hotel security cameras, the reluctance of some local store owners to let the family hang missing person posters and then more red tape in trying to gain access to her son's cellphone records.

"So many things should change to make it easier for people who go through this," she said. "We ask ourselves constantly, 'How much time was lost to red tape?'"

Then there are the people who write the story off to more crazy behavior from another out-of-control young adult. Problem is, there's no crazy behavior and no out-of-control adult. There's just this good kid—and few answers.

ELIZABETH

"Nude lying face up in bed. Beaten. Neck stabbed. Sexually assaulted. Strangled to death."

The facts on the police report are brutally chilling.

"Blood drops on bathroom floor. Adhesive substance on wrists. Numerous cut hairs on upper body and on bedding."

And it goes on.

Elizabeth Mae Hoffschneider was murdered in Huntington Beach on November 14, 1984. Just thirty-eight years old, her body was discovered in her Parkside Lane apartment by co-workers from the Fountain Valley medical company where she worked. Recently divorced, Hoffschneider was living alone. Huntington Beach detectives questioned many of the people in her life but made no arrests.

Detective Mike Reilly was a rookie patrol officer back then, and this became his first homicide case. He worked this case as well as he could, but to no avail. Even after this became a cold case, Reilly told me he never stopped thinking about it—could never get this victim out of his mind. "That's the problem," he said. "People forget victims. But they have families. They have friends. You cannot forget these people."

The police report I'm reading lists more details, marking the years that have gone by since the crime. "Case assigned to Detective Mike Reilly. Missing evidence found stored in separate police building. 2007: hairs collected from crime scene sent to Orange County Crime Lab. Hairs do not appear to be cut hairs as reported in 1984."

The plot thickens. "Several hairs have root follicles and are sent for DNA testing." Testing that was not available at the time of the crime.

The apartment where Elizabeth Mae Hoffschneider was murdered in 1984.

Then, the kicker: "2007: Lab identifies male DNA profile on three hairs. DNA eliminates all prior suspects. October 2007, CODIS hit." CODIS is a computer software program that operates local, state and national databases of DNA profiles from convicted offenders, unsolved crime scene evidence and missing persons.

Reilly's tenacity paid off.

The DNA matched a person in the California criminal database named Gerald Go, who was never even a suspect. Go's DNA was recorded because he was a felon; in 1986, he was convicted of assault and attempted rape in Costa Mesa. However, Go fled California before sentencing. For seventeen years, he ran loose until being arrested in New York in October 2004. He was brought back to California to serve his sentence, and as a condition of his parole, he had to provide DNA samples. Ironically, had Go served his sentence in 1987, DNA samples would not have been required.

After the DNA hit, the HBPD released this news: "An Orange County fugitive was arrested this week in Toronto, Canada, for the 1984 murder of a Huntington Beach woman. Gerald Su Go, 51, is charged with murder with allegations for murder during the commission of rape, burglary and robbery. If convicted, he faces a maximum sentence of life without the possibility of parole. He was arrested on a warrant by Toronto Police on Oct. 25, 2007, and will face extradition proceedings in Canada."

That's where it stands now—waiting to get this man back to Huntington Beach to face trial.

The facts of this case, along with details of the spectacular police work, are well documented.

But what I wanted to include, after talking to surviving family members and to Reilly, is how lucky we are to have a detective of this caliber in our community. When I first contacted him, he made it clear—focus on the victim, not him. And that's what I wanted to do. I spoke with several of her family members, and what emerged are memories of a vibrant young woman who suffered the worst of fates at the hands of a sadistic predator. To see her photo today, it breaks one's heart to think of what these people have had to endure the last twenty-five years.

"Somebody took my beautiful sister." "I cry almost every day." "I see her in all of the young women I pass every day."

Their pain is palpable, and they don't want their sister to be forgotten.

The family members also talk of Reilly, who never gave up, who gave them comfort and who delivered the goods. Reilly, who wins awards, who is spoken of by associates in the noblest of terms and who does not want any attention.

"It never seems to get printed, how many people these crimes affect," he said. "But we have to remember them. Also, a lot of people did some terrific work on this case. That's how we got this guy. Along with the science of DNA."

The column this week is dedicated to the lasting memory of Elizabeth Mae Hoffschneider, a Huntington Beach woman whose tragic death we mourn along with her family. It's also dedicated to Detective Mike Reilly, who (whether he likes it or not) deserves a ton of grateful admiration. Excellent work, Detective Reilly. We're proud of you.

As well, this column will stay on this case as it progresses toward justice.

MEN ON A MOUNTAIN

For this upcoming Memorial Day, I present the story of two men.

One is searching for a path back in time to touch the spirit of his father.

The other wants to help him get there.

Ron Grubbs lost his dad at four years old. The Grubbses were stationed at the Marine Corps Air Station in El Toro. On November 18, 1950, Ron's dad, First Lieutenant Willard M. "Bill" Grubbs, was part of a four-man flight aboard a USMC Beechcraft SNB-5. The plane was returning to El Toro

Pat Macha with a map indicating where many plane crash sites are around Orange County.

from Arizona on a routine training flight. The skies in Orange County were thick with clouds, heavy rain and gusty winds. With his wife and two young children waiting for him to come home, tragically, Bill Grubbs perished as the plane crashed into the mountains above Mission Viejo.

Pat Macha, a longtime Huntington Beach resident (who moved to Mission Viejo a couple years ago), has been locating downed aircraft in remote regions for more than forty years. He's trudged to more than eight hundred sites all over the world, looking primarily for military wrecks. Since the early 1980s, he's also made it his mission to deliver the next of kin to many of these sites so that they can make private peace where loved ones gave their lives. "I wasn't in the service," the retired high school teacher told me recently. "But I had many family members who were. Maybe this is my way of serving my country."

Macha has become quite well known for his selfless missions, which is how he arrived on Ron Grubbs's radar. Soon after contacting Macha from his home in St. Louis, Ron Grubbs (along with his wife, Aileen) finds himself in a four-wheel drive vehicle, rumbling up a precarious dirt road, climbing higher and higher into the dusty Santa Ana Mountains. (The team also includes myself; Park Ranger Tom Maloney; Deborah Clarke; the USFS Trabuco Ranger District Trails manager, Pete Armes; and Carol Ohman and Greg Robertson, a pair of siblings whose uncle was also killed in the crash.)

We park several hundred feet beneath the crash site. The morning is unseasonably warm and breezy; a bright yellow sun beats strong in a blue, cloudless sky. Before our ascent, Ron Grubbs takes a deep breath and stares up at the rocks where the plane hit.

"After fifty-nine years," he says, "it's surreal to be here. I'm not sure what I'll find, but as a son, I just finally had to do this."

As fit as he and his wife are, the climb will not be easy. We are warned about ticks, dehydration, poison oak, bees and especially rattlesnakes, which is why each of us probes ahead of each step with a hiking stick.

On a steep incline, like so many goats, we start the slow march upward across the rugged terrain. Pat Macha explains that were it not for the fires of 2007, this trek would be impossible due to deep growth. But for all the brush that the fires cleared, the chaparral is starting to come back with a swift, beautiful vengeance. Bright green, yellow, purple and orange wildflowers, including yucca, chickweed, goldenstars and deer weed, give way to thousands of ivory-colored morning glories brushed with traces of buttery yellow. The flowers look innocent enough—that is, until their knotty vines begin tripping us up at the ankles. "They're also called 'bind weeds,'" chuckles Maloney.

Baby-stepping our way a couple hundred yards up, mini-avalanches start to occur as thick grasses transition into dirt and soft rock near the summit. Up here, plump emerald- and ruby-colored hummingbirds dart and buzz by our heads in the hot wind. Sharp-green yucca leaves stab at our calves. "Spanish daggers," Maloney smiles.

When we reach the primary debris field, Macha pushes aside dirt and picks up pieces of plane. Large, rusty, twisted pieces of metal rest near dozens of other smaller fragments including belt buckles, parachute harnesses, wires, small plates of metal with serial numbers—much was recovered, but much remains. Macha narrates calmly and carefully what everything is (he came to this site for the first time in 1965). Then he pulls out the American flags he ceremoniously places at spots like this.

Ron Grubbs is wearing his dad's watch and a ring, both artifacts recovered at the site. "They came down the mountain once, and now they've come back up," he says.

Ron Grubbs stands at the site where his father lost his life in 1950.

Then Grubbs makes a poignant speech and places a flag on a piece of wreckage. He also leaves a small container for his dad, filled with pictures of grandkids Bill Grubbs never got to hold—and a letter he wrote to his dad. Finally, and dramatically, he produces a small vial containing some of his mom's ashes and spreads them across the hill, intertwining the memory of his parents, Bill and Bernice, for eternity.

We stand where the debris settled, but the precise impact site is perhaps another one hundred feet above us, up a slightly treacherous ledge. Ron has made it this far and wants to continue the ascent.

So up we go.

At nearly five thousand feet, we reach the summit where the plane crashed. A giant yellow cross, painted on the impact boulder in the 1950s, still remains. Ron reflects more from on high. He recalls how his dad taught him about the planes at El Toro—and the event that brings us here today.

"You know," he says, "in November 1950, my mom was with the other wives—in one NAMAR housing unit—waiting.

"The marines brought a big Turkey dinner on one night, it was around Thanksgiving, and they all just stared at it. And the marines took it away.

Then, after three days, someone said, 'Here comes the Brass.' And they all knew, at that moment, it was over."

Soon, we are back at the vehicles. Preparing to leave the scene, Ron Grubbs gives the mountaintop one more wistful glance as his wife gives him a hug.

Someone commends Macha for arranging trips like this. "I'm just here as a grateful citizen of the republic," he shrugs. "This is the least I can do to help others pay their respects."

This is the story of two men: one who journeyed and found peace high on a mountain, where a craggy granite pinnacle cradles and protects the memory of his father. And another, a "grateful citizen of the republic" who made the journey possible.

This Memorial Day, to all the men and women who gave their lives serving the United States of America, may we bow our heads—and remember.

ABOUT THE AUTHOR

C hris Epting is an award-winning music and travel journalist and author of over twenty pop culture books, including *Led Zeppelin Crashed Here: The Locations of America's Rock and Roll Landmarks*, *Roadside Baseball*, *James Dean Died Here* and several history books about Huntington Beach and Orange County. He has written his "In the Pipeline" for the *Huntington Beach Independent* newspaper since 2007. Originally from New York, Chris lives in Huntington Beach with his wife and two children. Visit www.chrisepting. com for more information, or follow Chris on Twitter: @chrisepting.